གནས་ཡུལ་ཇི་ནའོ། ཀྲུང་གོའི་ལྷ་ས་གྲོང་ཁྱེར་མི་རིགས་ལམ་ཁྲ་དཀྱིལ་དང་ཆོ། དར་ཤོག། 7391 ཁ་པར། 22221 23222

地址：中国拉萨民族路1号　电报：7391　电话：22221　23222

ADDRESS NO. 1 NATION ROAD LHASA CHINA CABLE: 7391　LHASA

CN TEL: 22221　23222

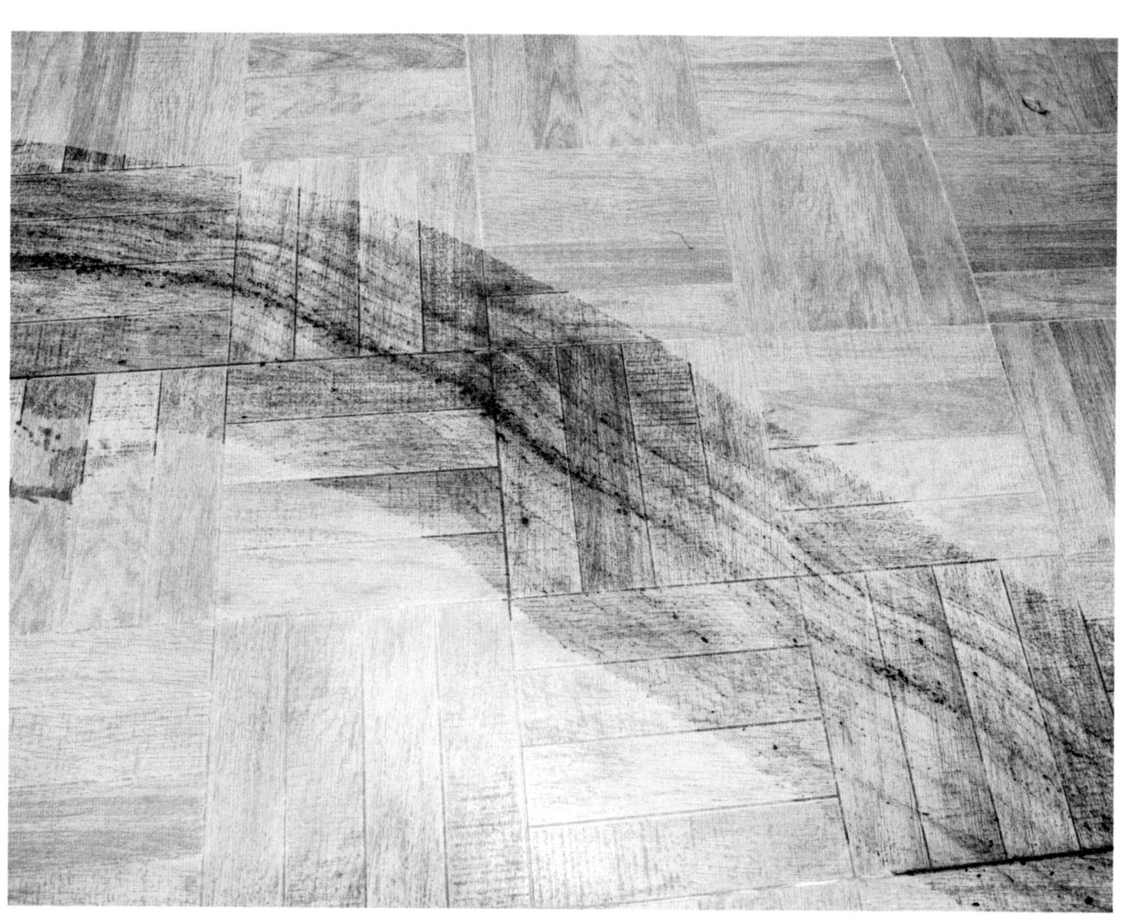

Tenzing Dakpa

Steidl

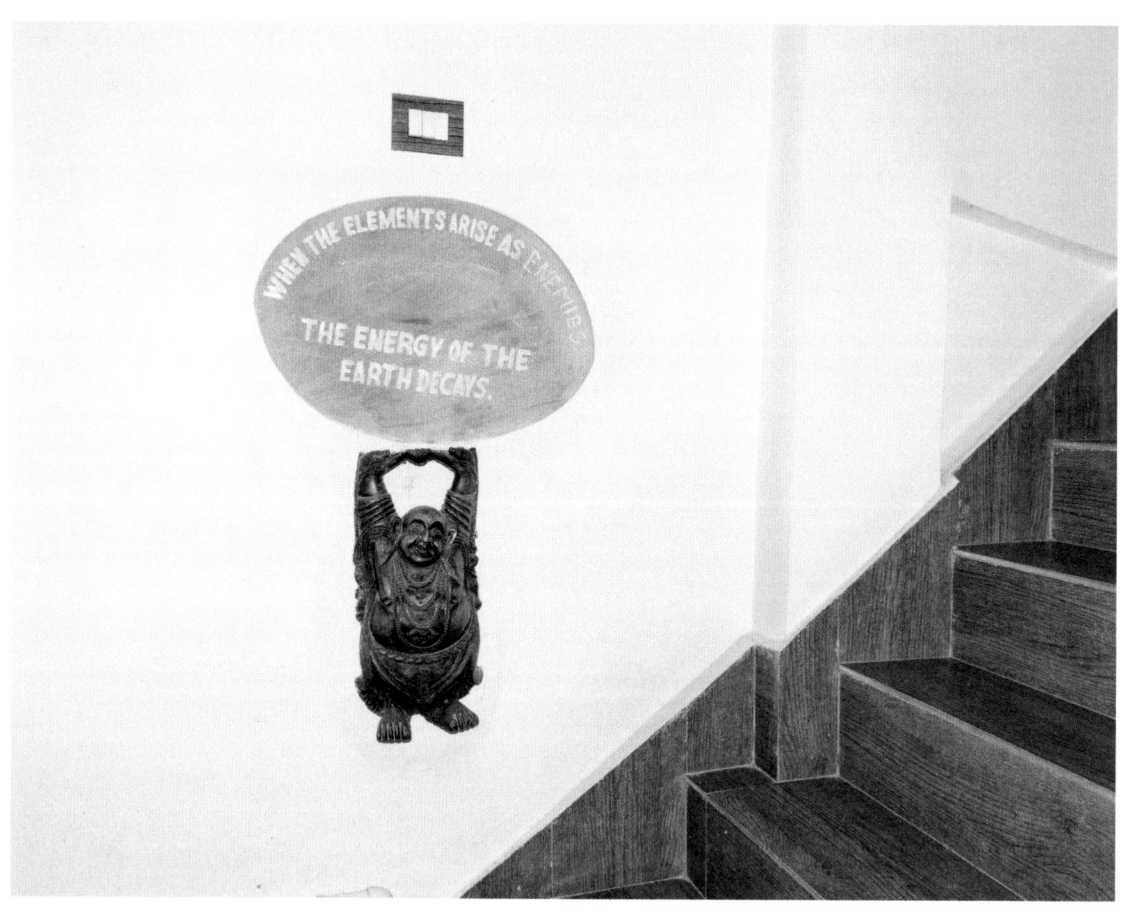
WHEN THE ELEMENTS ARISE AS ENEMIES
THE ENERGY OF THE
EARTH DECAYS.

for Pala and Amla

THE HOTEL

མཚན་ན་ཁང་།

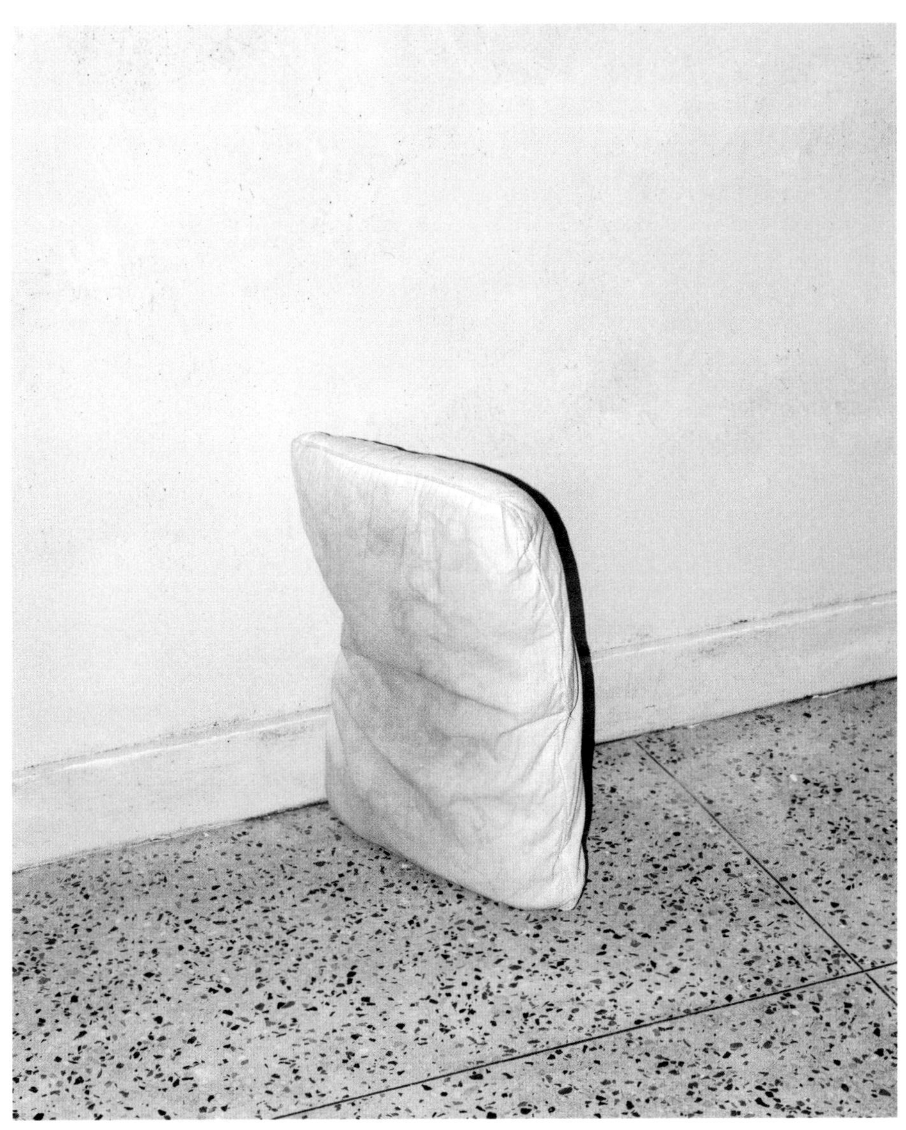

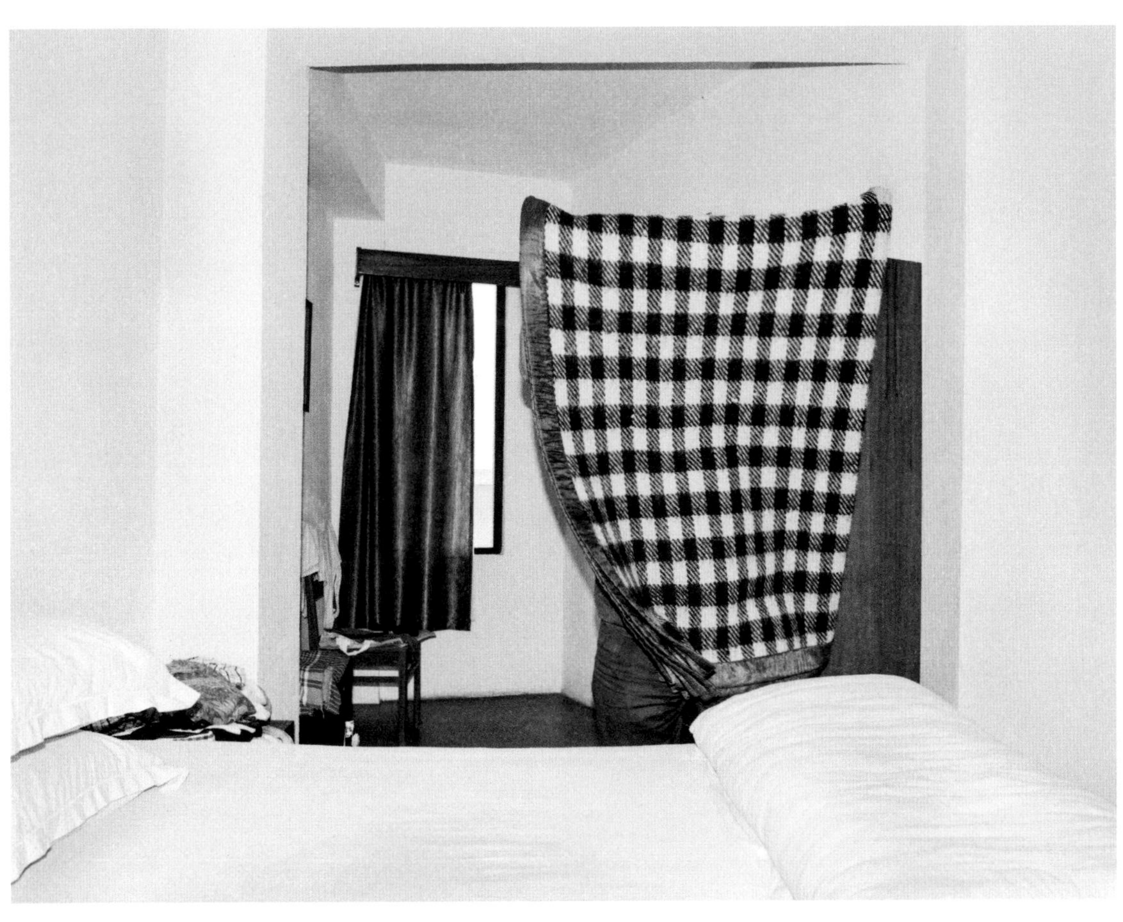

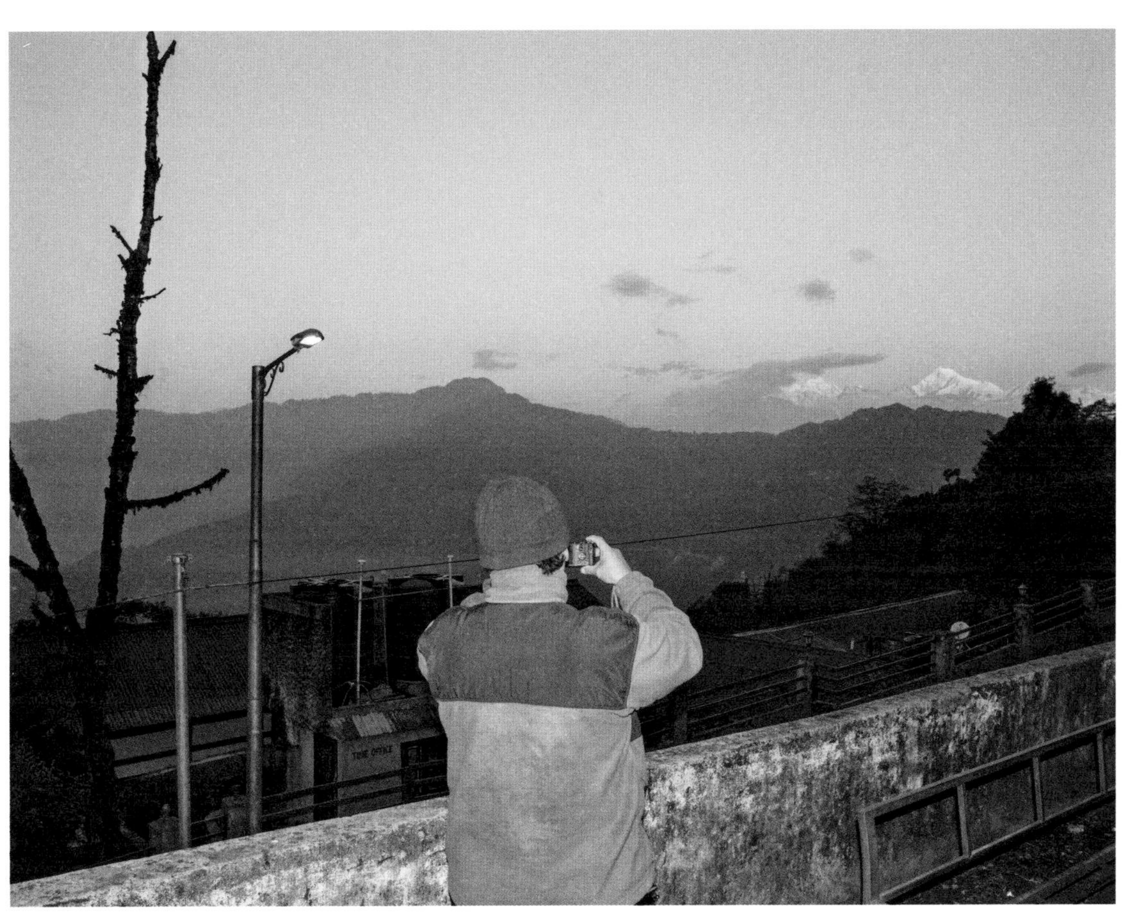

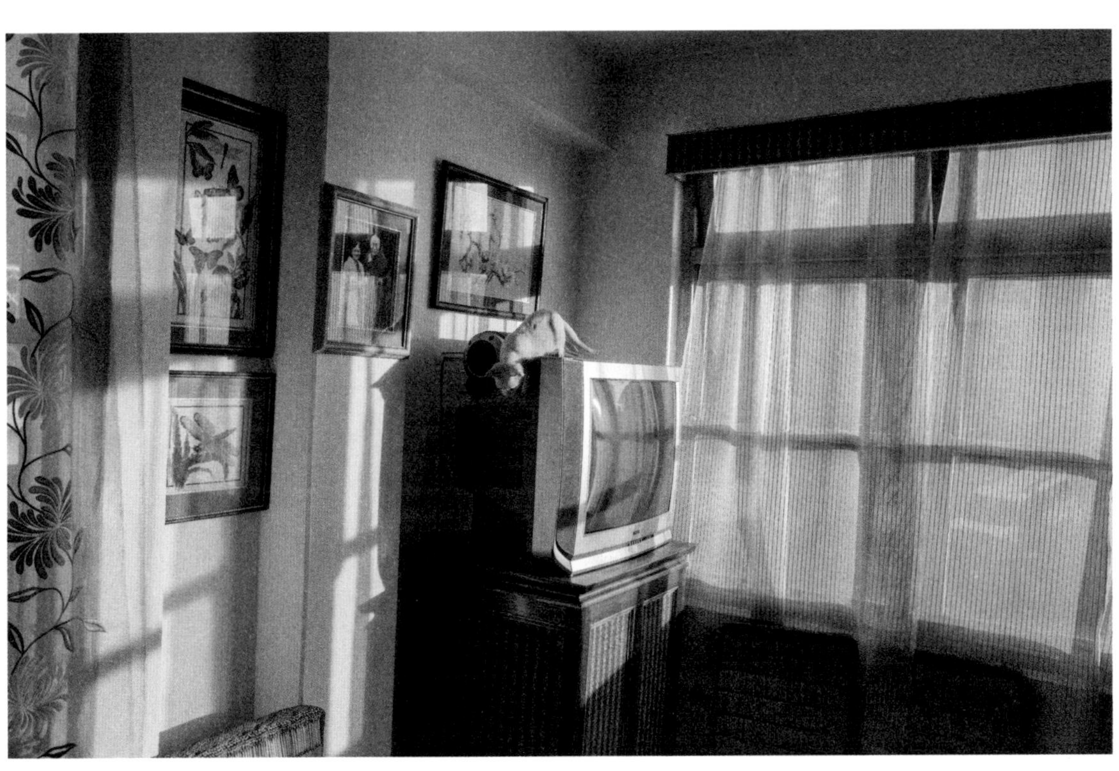

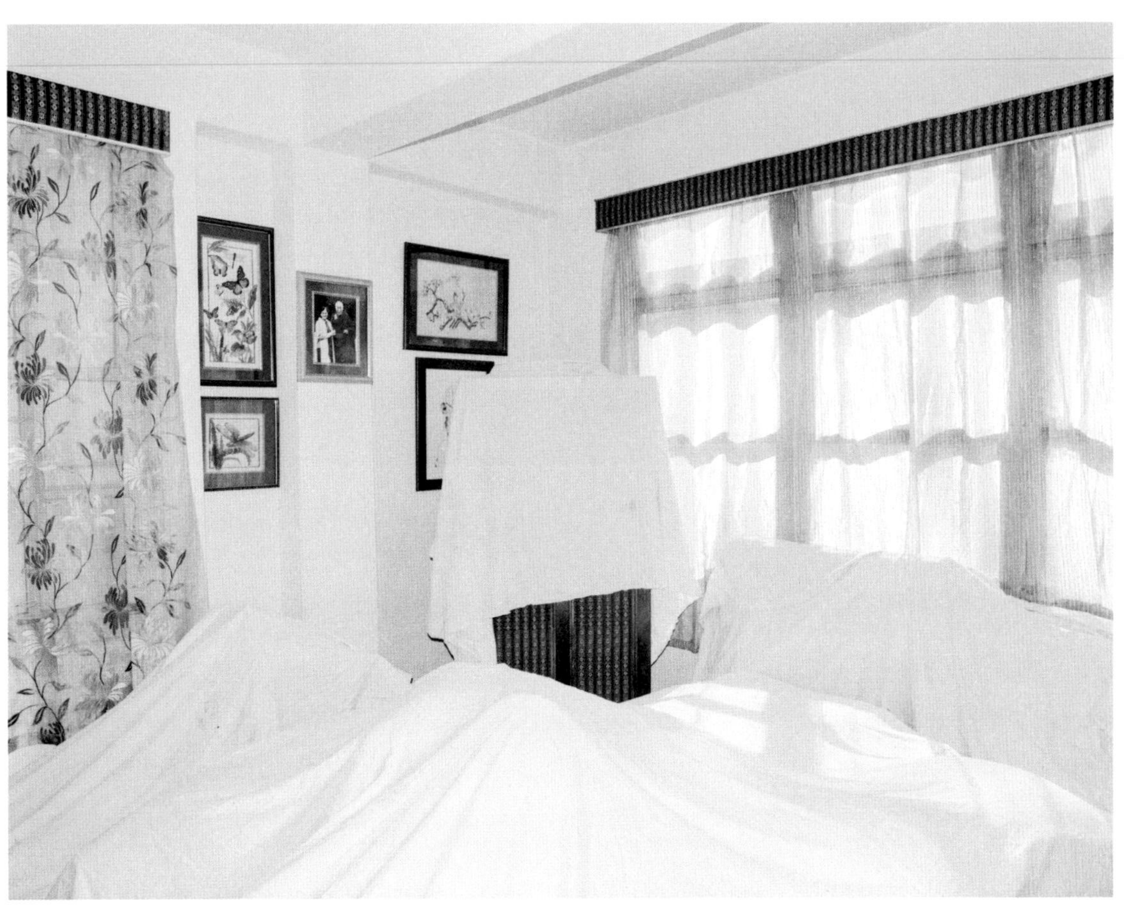

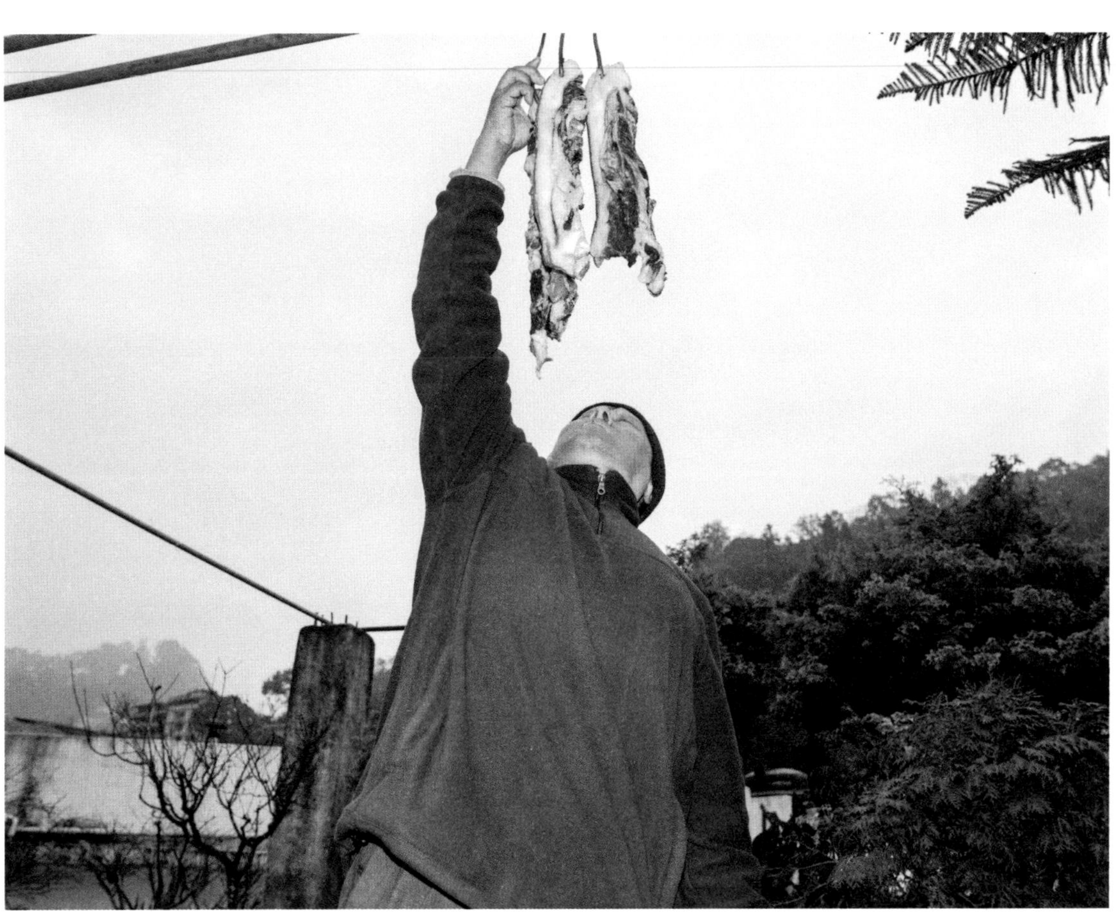

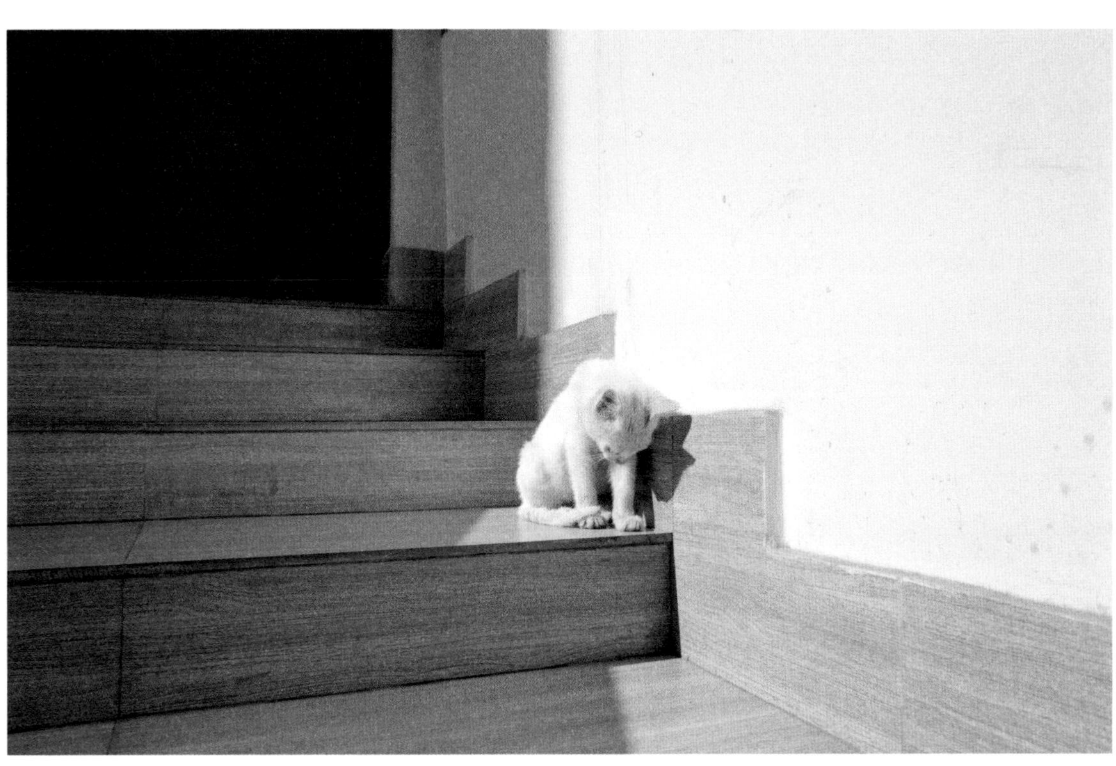

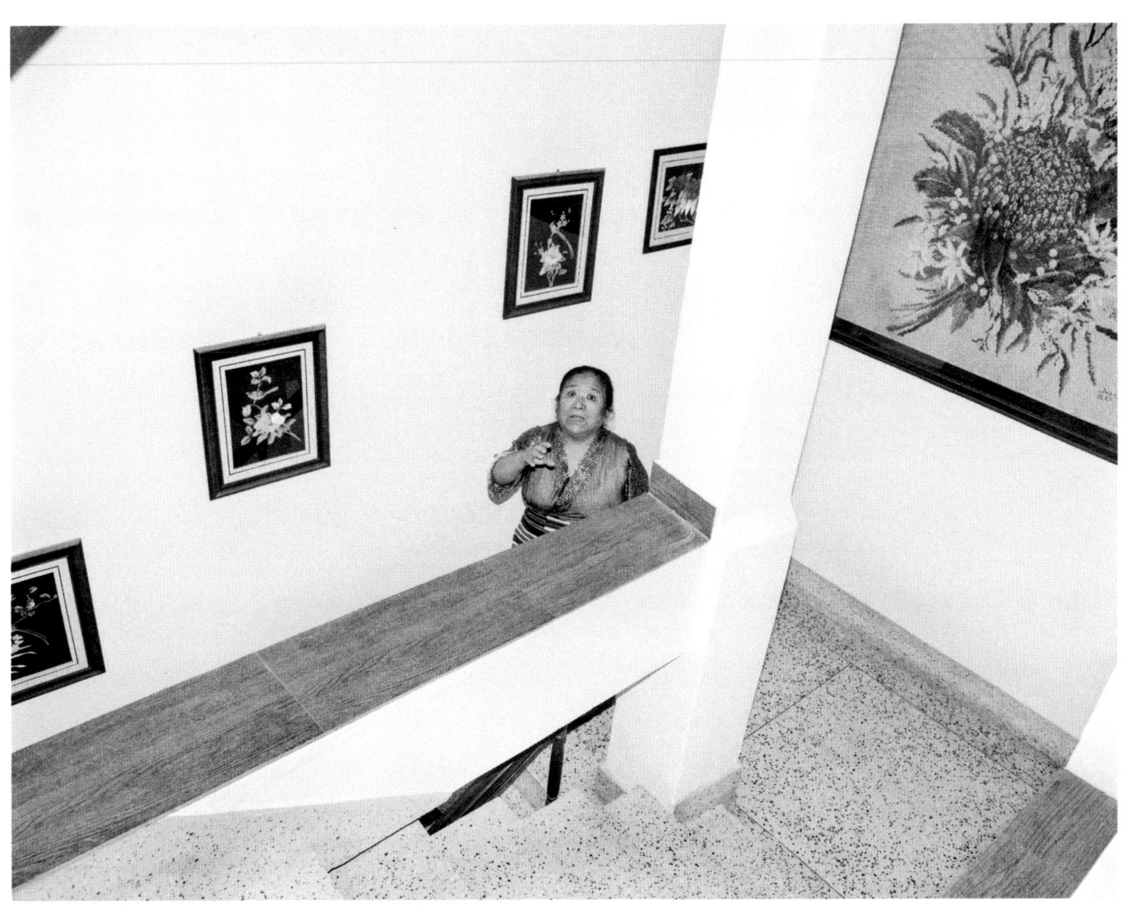

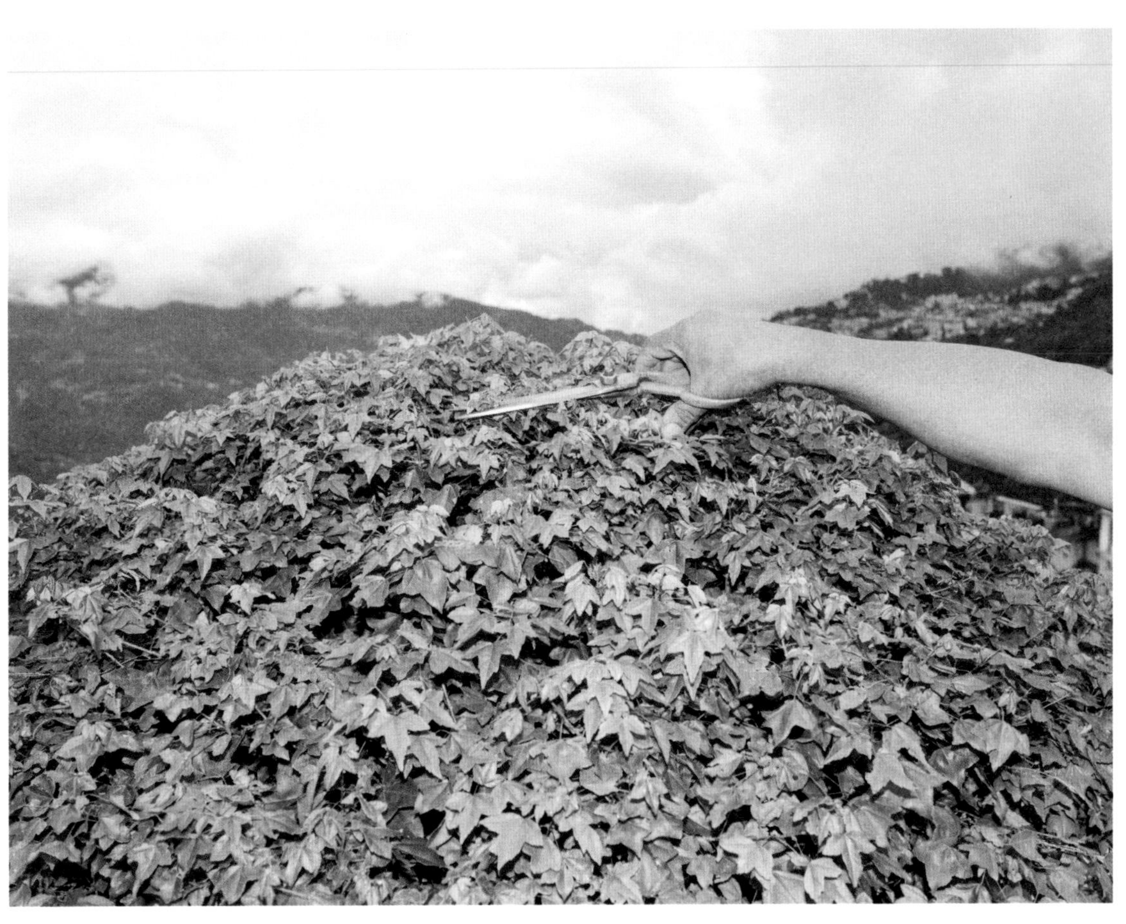

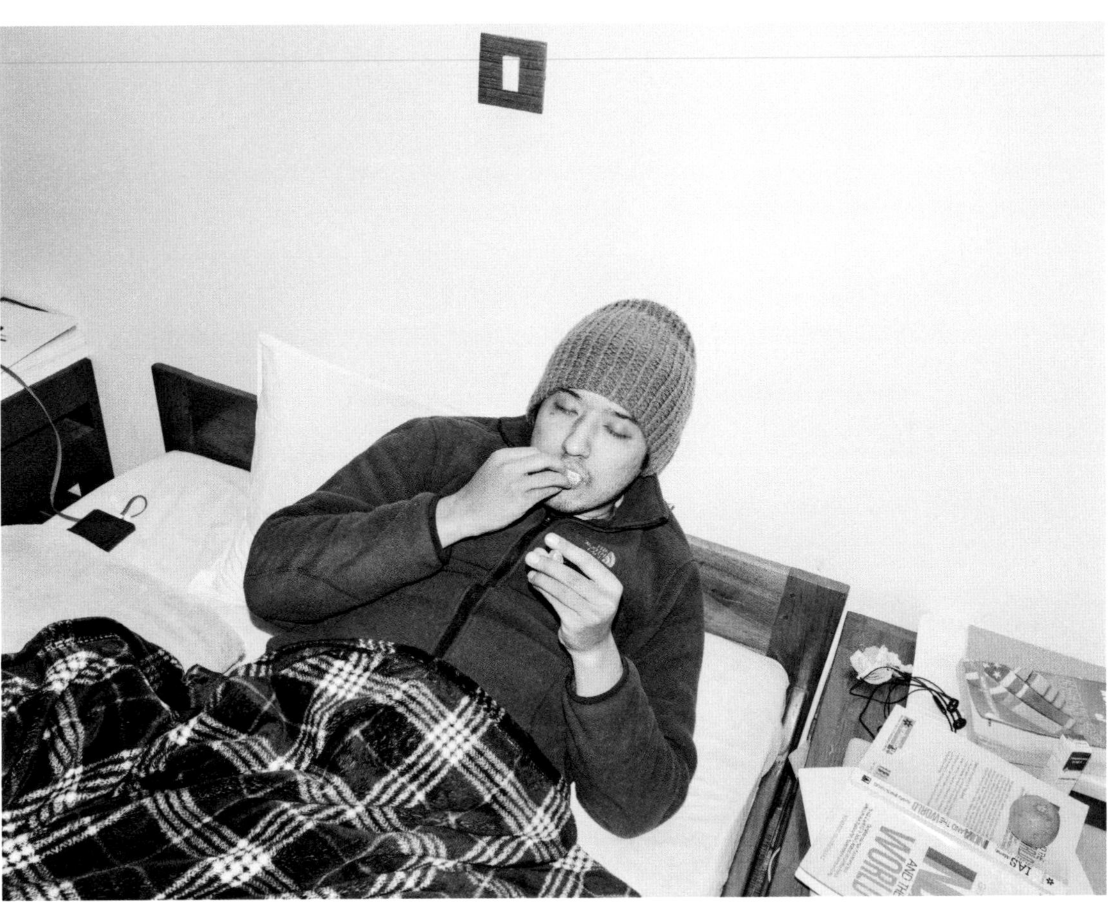

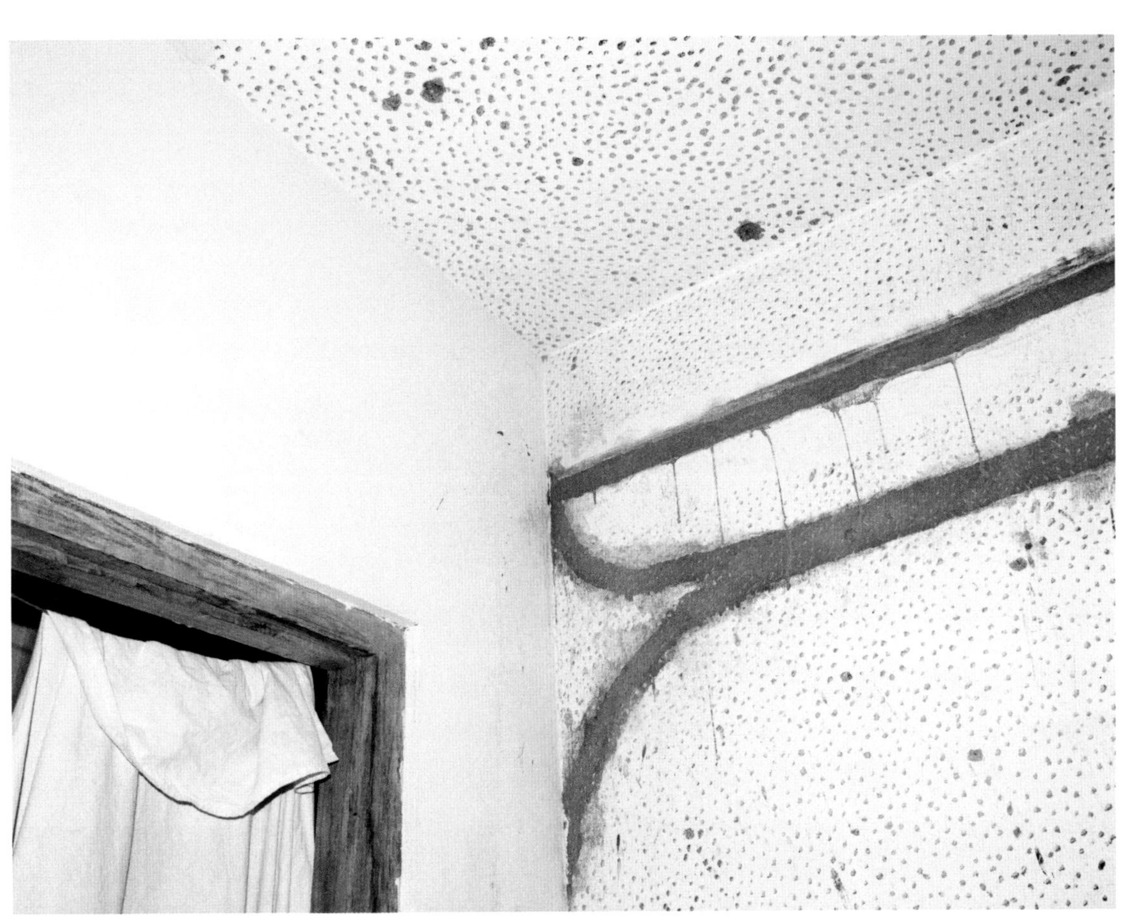

Family and Memory

My first vague memory of childhood is of me crawling on a prickly carpet of grass towards what I clearly remember was a jackfruit tree. In trying to retrace the memory I asked my father about this place. He says that it was in the garden in front of our house in Bhutan. My memory quickly tries to recalibrate to my place of birth and I ask my parents where was I born. They say in Kalimpong, West Bengal. This information brings back a vague memory of my foot getting swamped in a paddy field where I am stuck for a while. I lose my shoe, yet I don't remember how I manage to get out. Everything else is blank, until I remember being locked up in a cupboard for talking in a kindergarten class in Gangtok, Sikkim. My birth certificate says I was born on 21 November 1985 in Gangtok, Sikkim, although my aunts differ, saying I was born much earlier and that I'm older than their sons who were born in 1985. I remember having to change schools repeatedly and attend kindergarten for almost four years before I could pronounce words.

My father does not remember his date of birth and his Indian passport says 26 January 1955, which is the Republic Day of India. My mother's Indian passport states 2 October 1964, which is the day when Gandhi was born. Having asked my parents if the dates were coincidental, my dad jokingly said that he had to come up with a date; these are prominent national holidays in India.

I was always under the impression that my brother was a year older than me until I recently saw his documents, which state 1982 and that he was born in Gangtok. Yet my parents confirm that my brother was born in Kalimpong in one of the best maternity hospitals during those times, pointing out of the car window, at what was now a dilapidated old pile of concrete.

The nature of our official identity and place on paper is adopted and the one which is in our memory is fragmented, revealed only in places we once remember.

Looking at photographs from the old family album adds a deeper complexity to our history. It shows my mother in her early teens, group portraits of her family in Tibetan attire, my paternal grandfather in an HMIS British Indian Navy uniform from 1942, and pictures of my father from his childhood and teenage years in a landscape that could be anywhere between Bhutan and Kalimpong.

My mother was born in Bhutan and spent most of her younger years there. She recounts attending Tibetan boarding schools in India for a few years, which she disliked. My maternal grandparents, traders by occupation, come from the southern part of Tibet. After Tibet's annexation in 1959, fearing for their lives, a large section of the community migrated to Bhutan and different parts of India. Now and then my mother reminisces about her childhood days in the apple orchards of Bhutan.

After a surge of political tensions and pressure from the Bhutanese government in the early eighties, the Tibetan community from Bhutan was forced to leave. My parents along with my grandmother then moved to Sikkim and in the following years started a restaurant business. Their life since has been invested in maintaining and providing service and hospitality to the guests who come and stay in the hotel.

Tenzing Dakpa

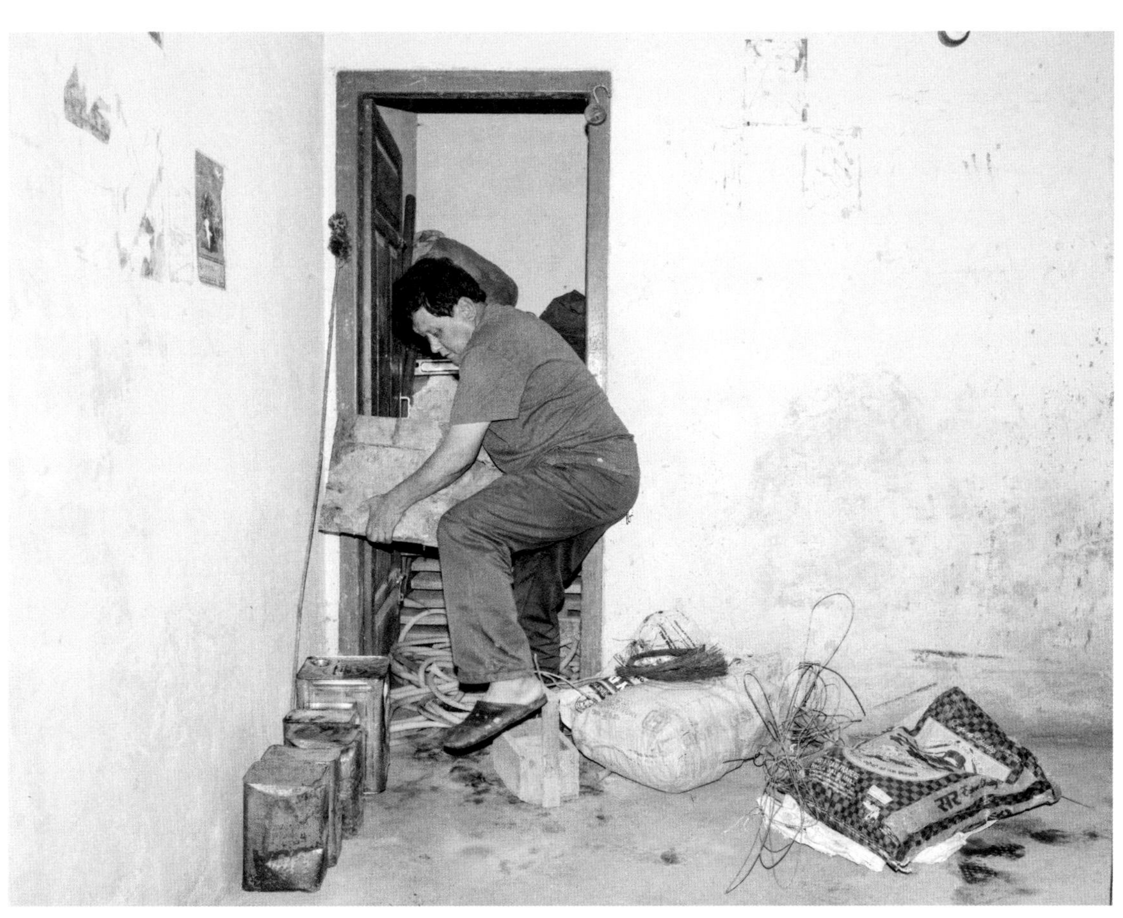

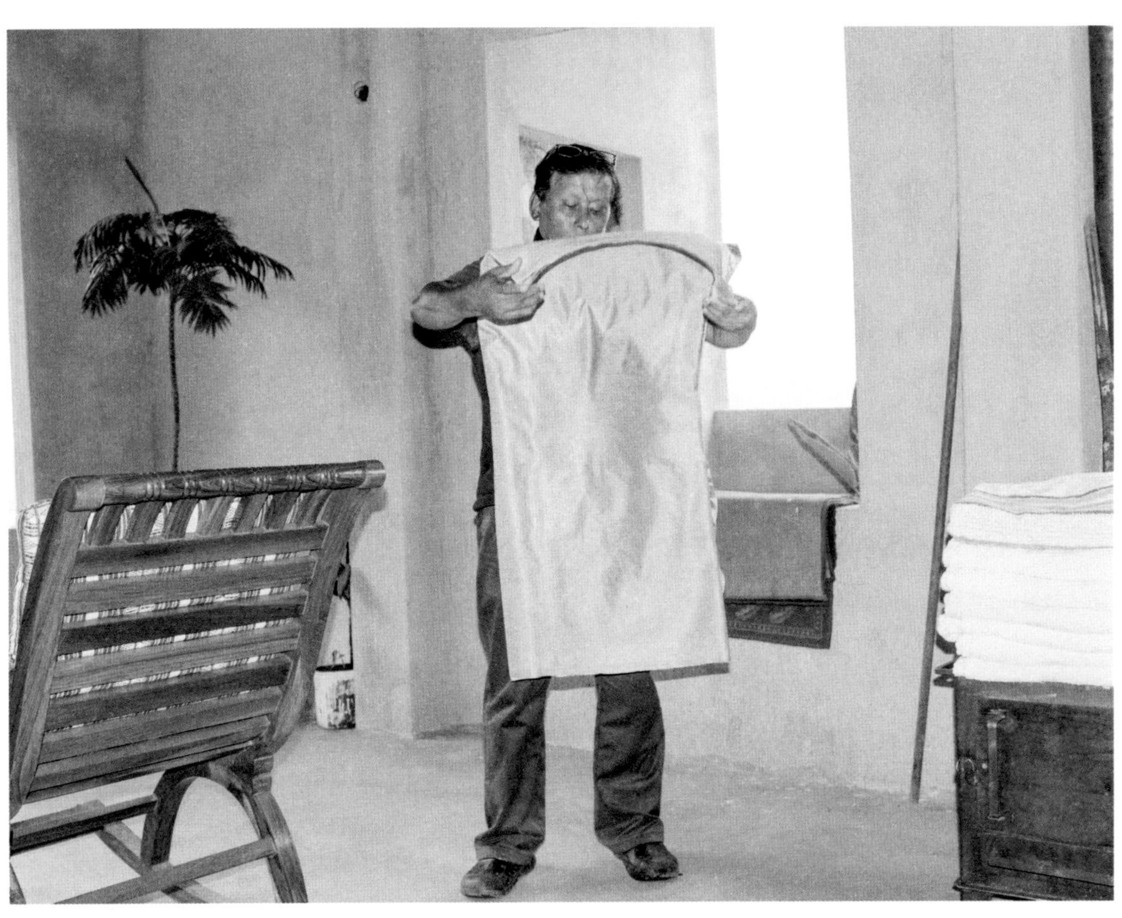

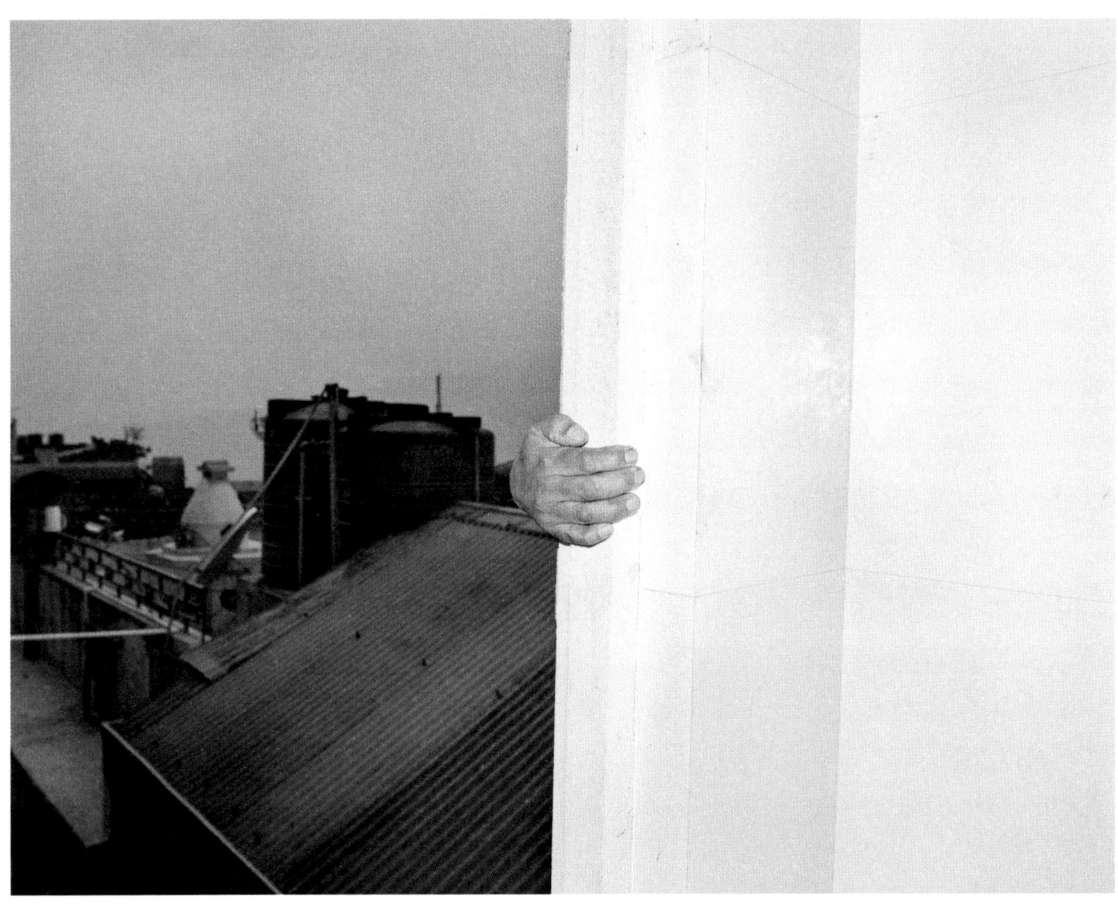

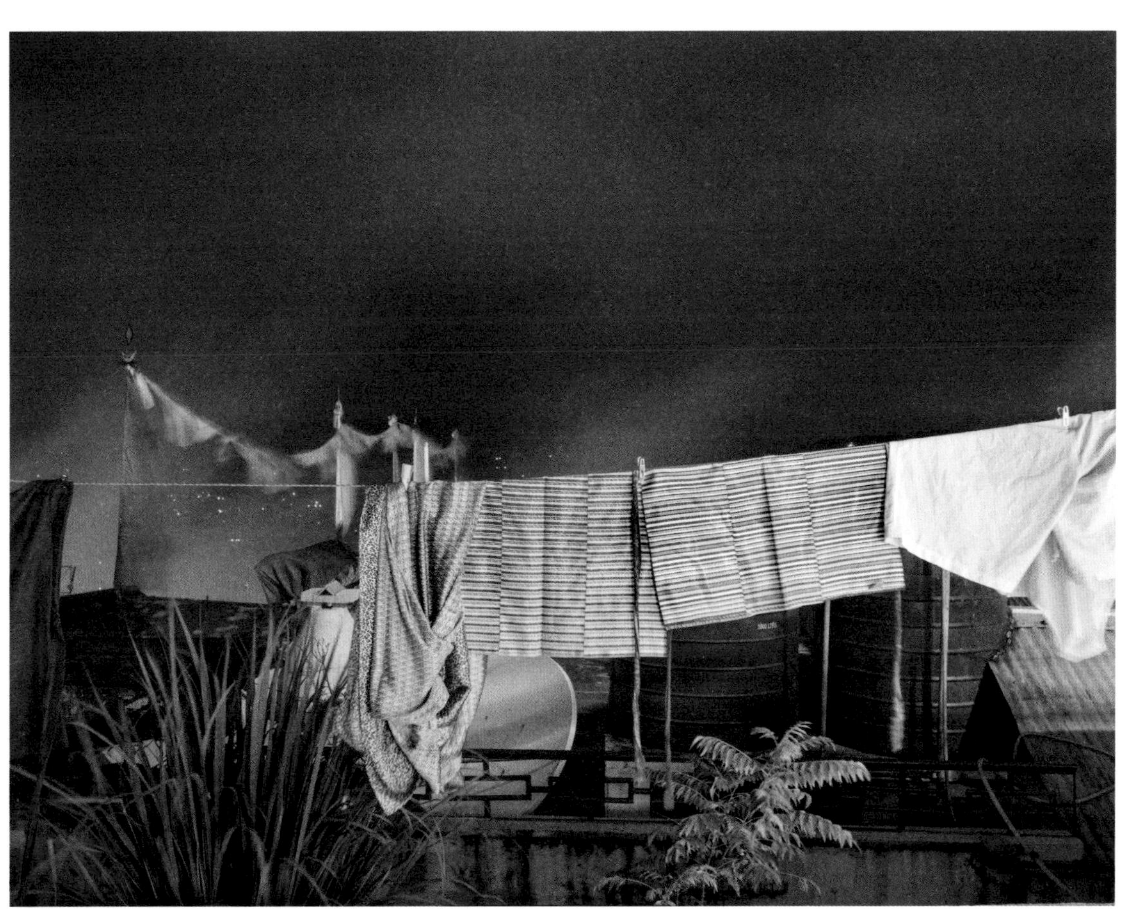

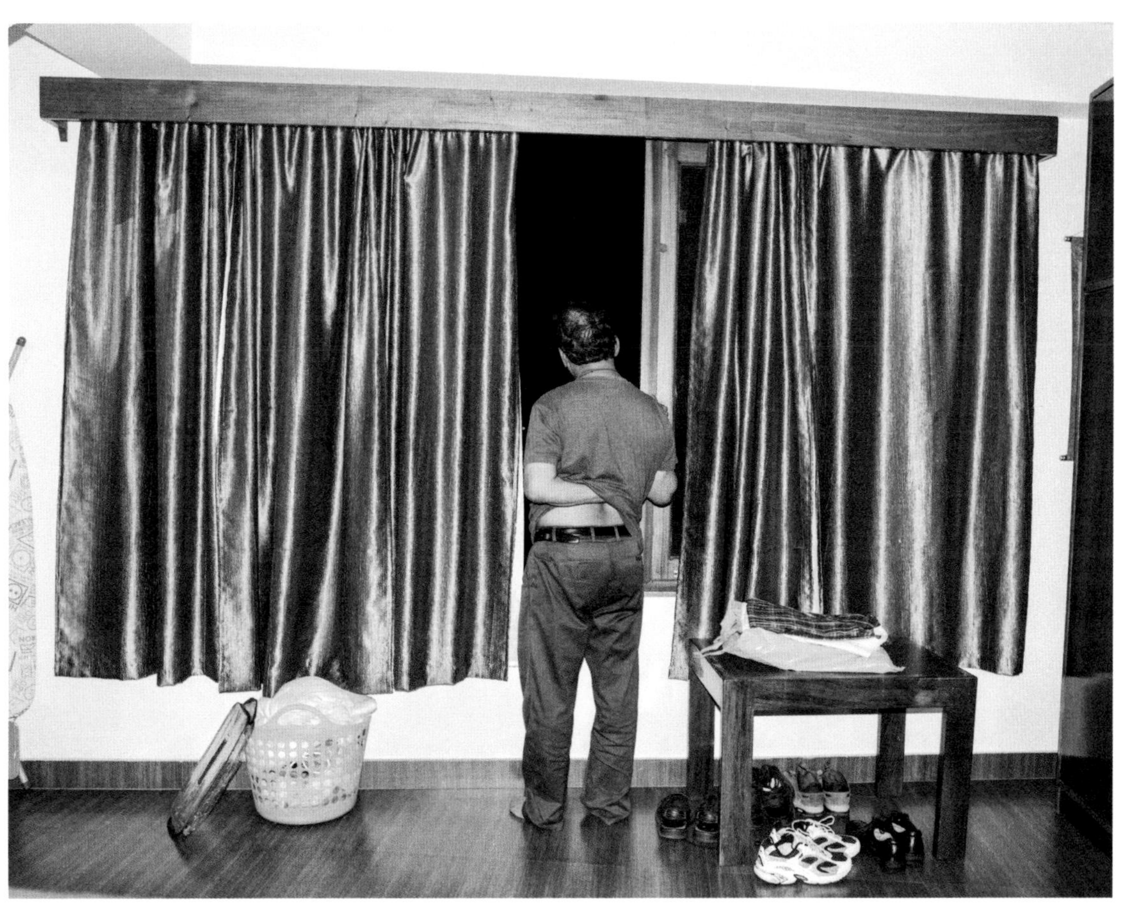

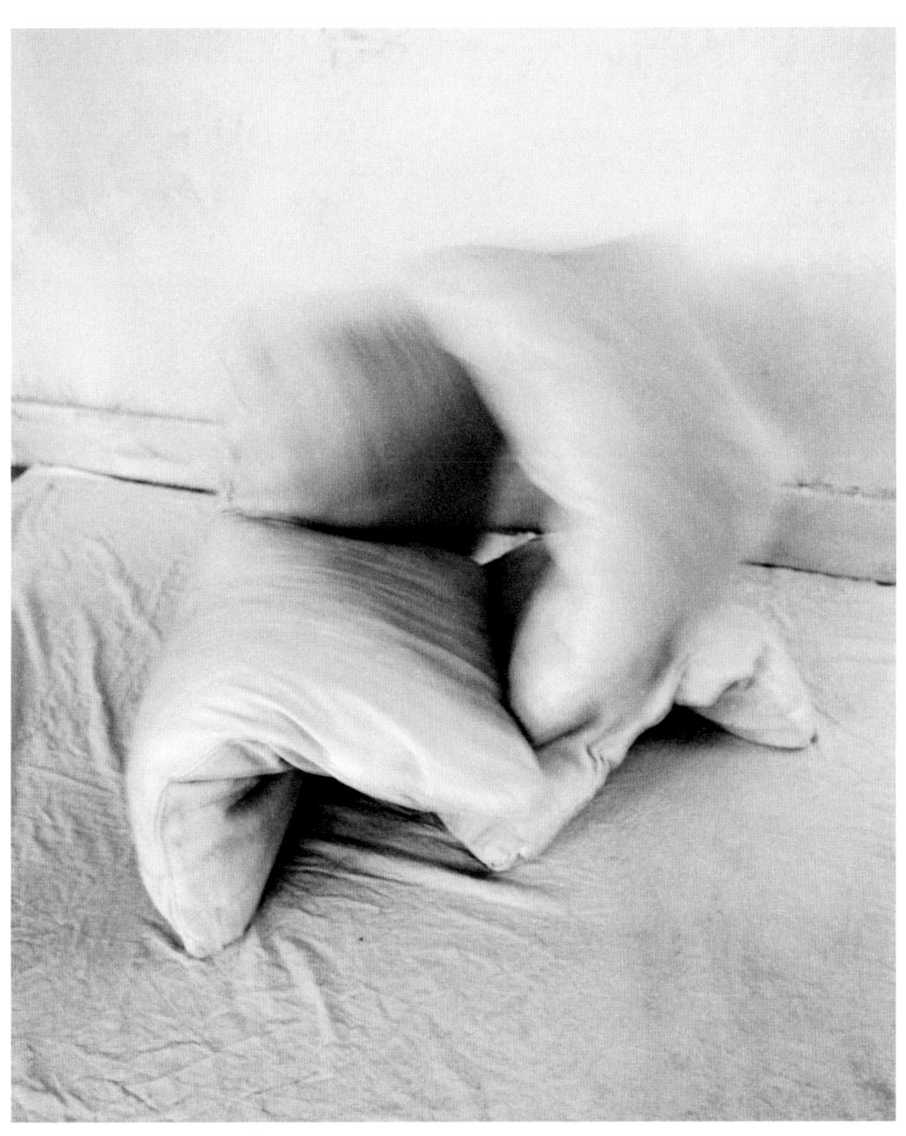

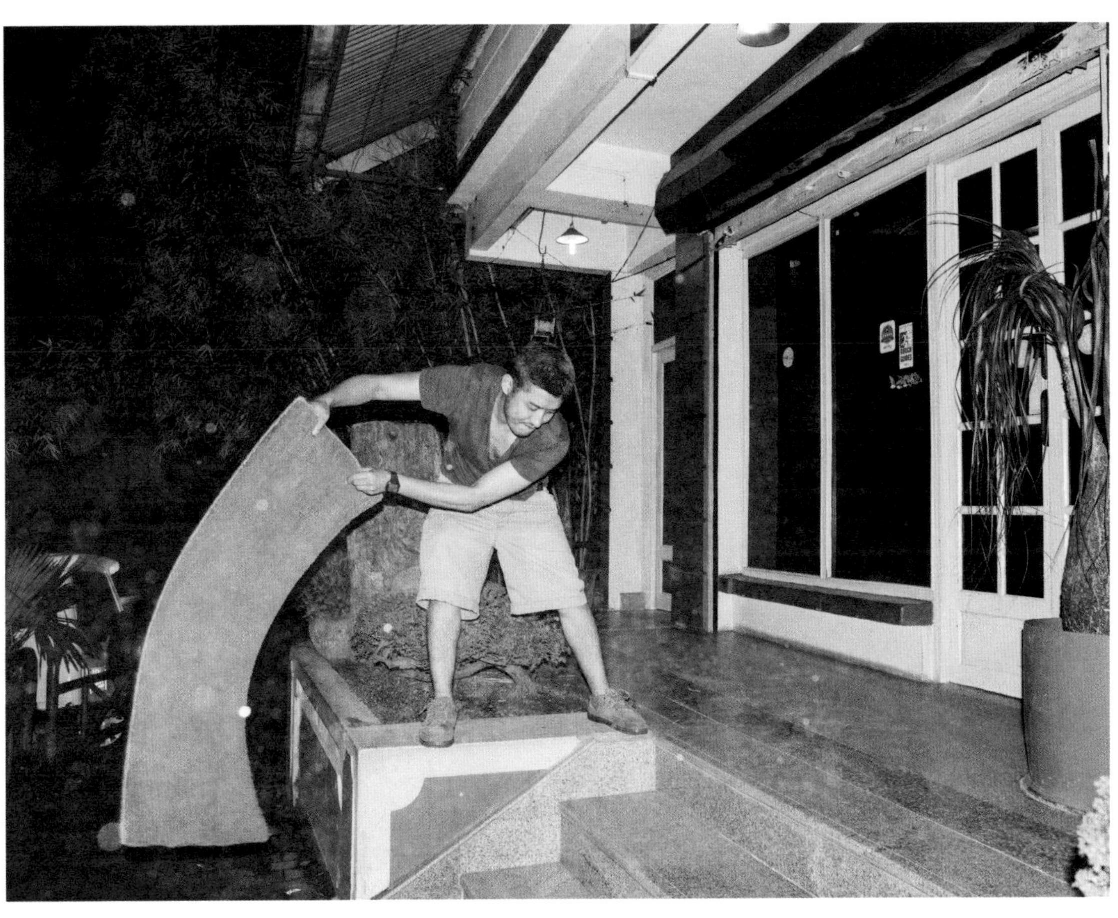

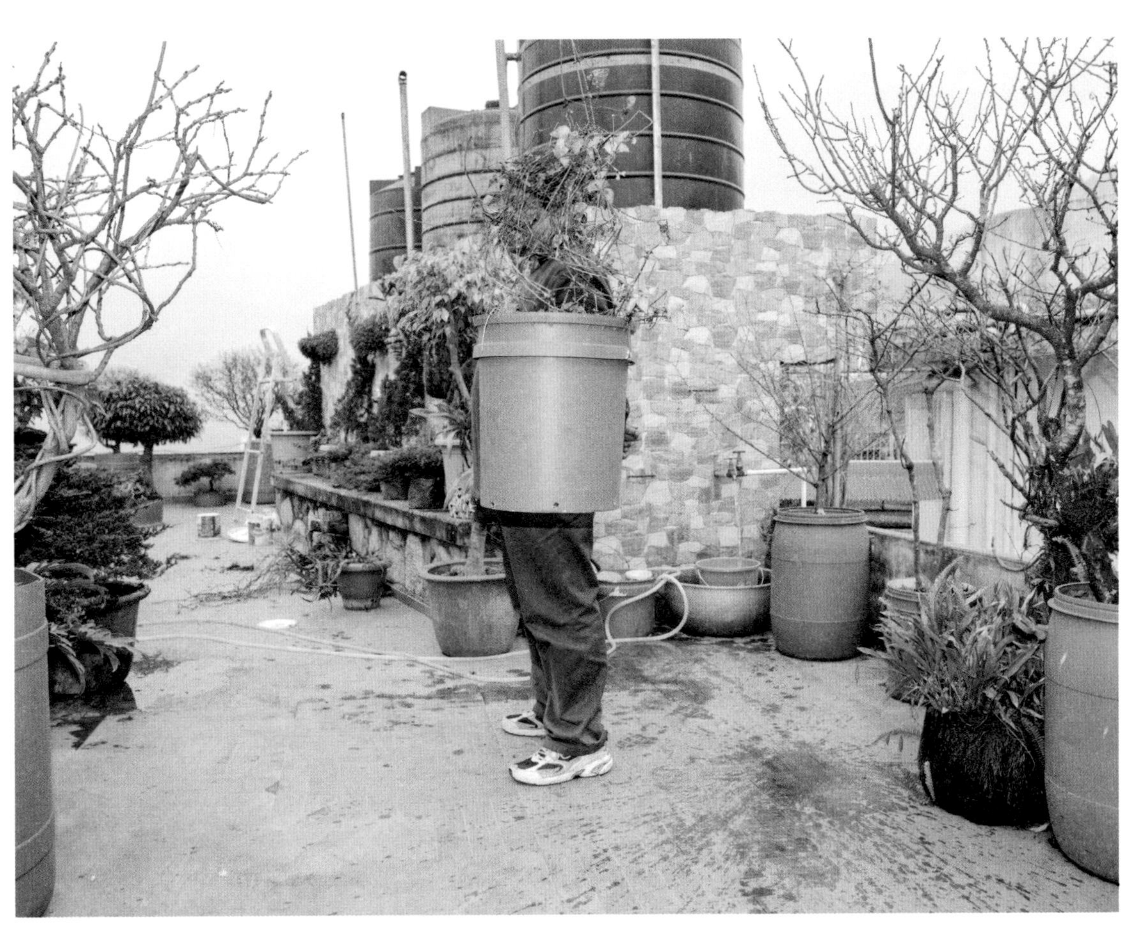

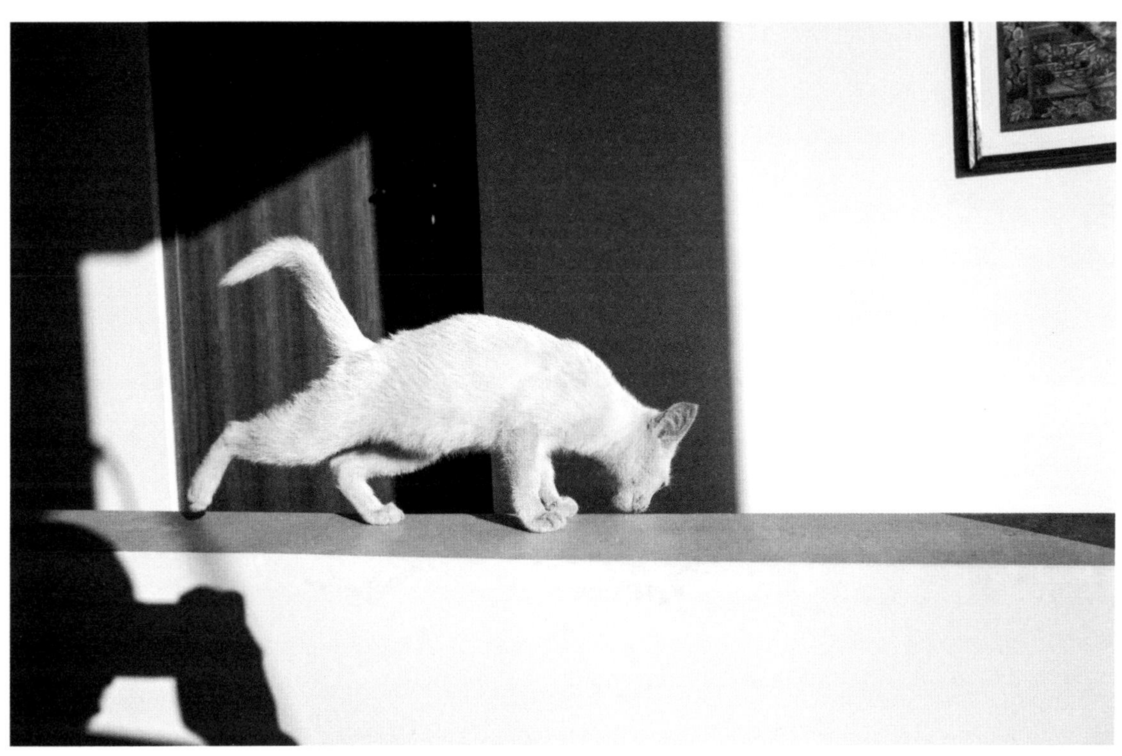

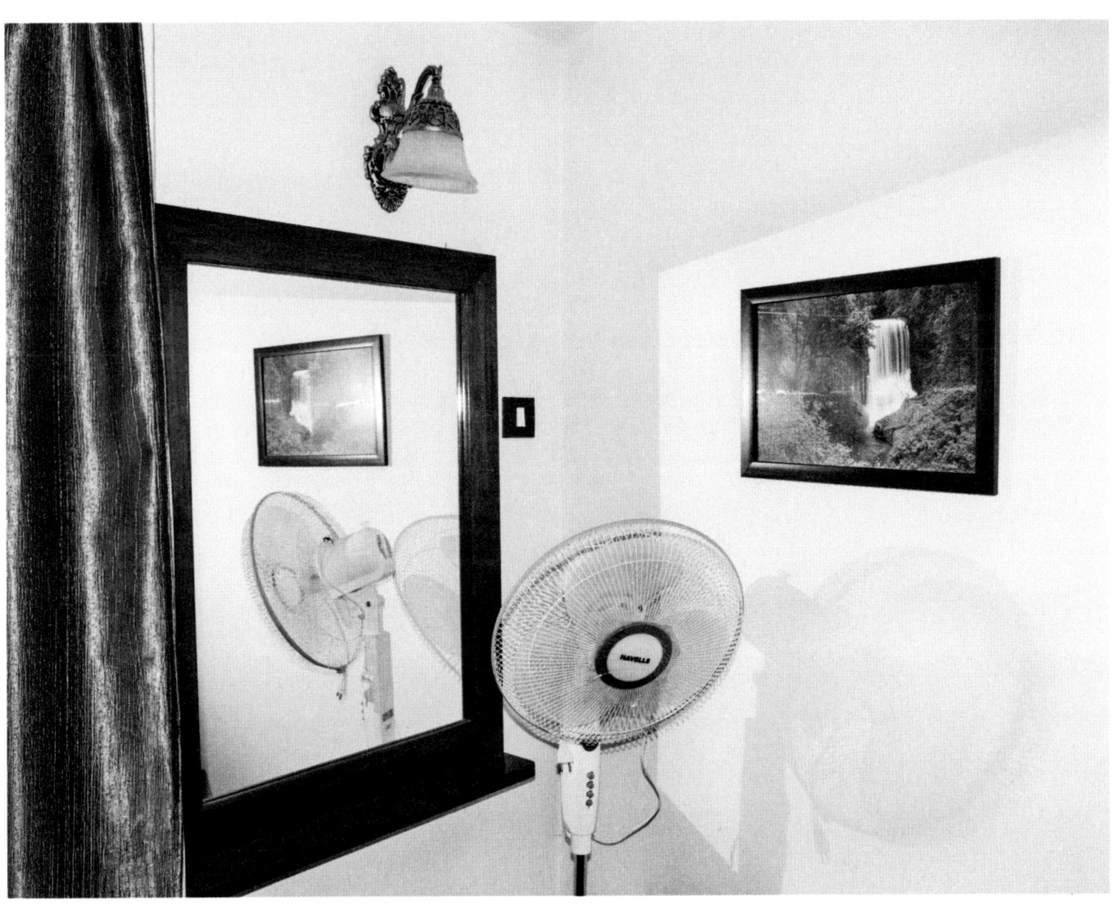

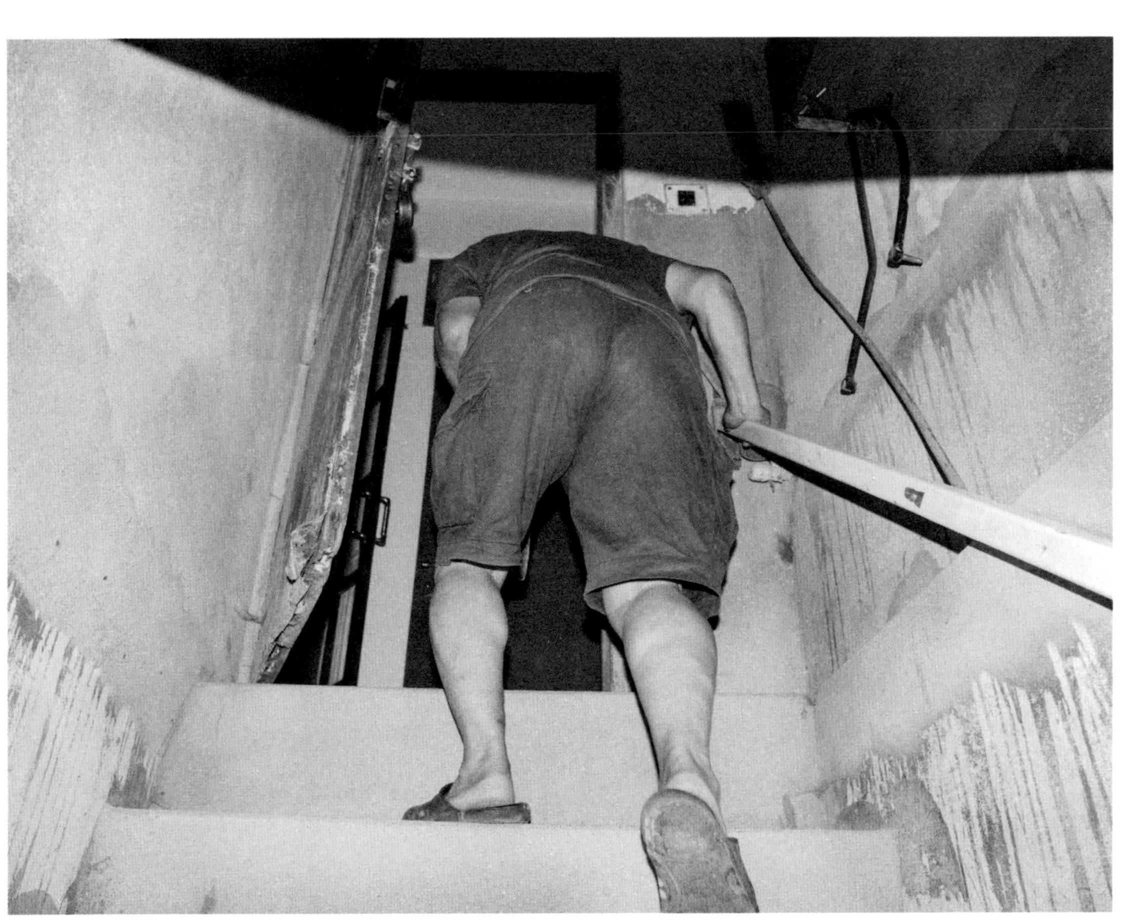

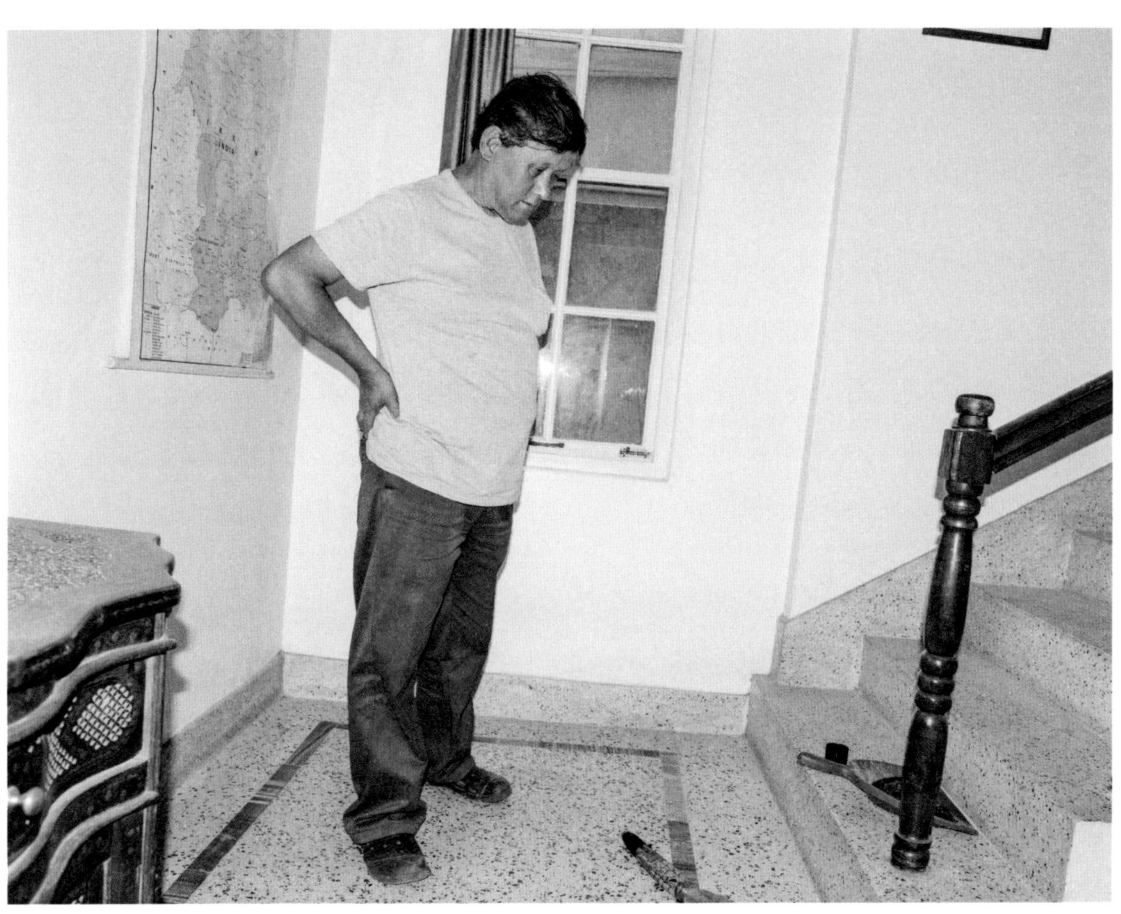

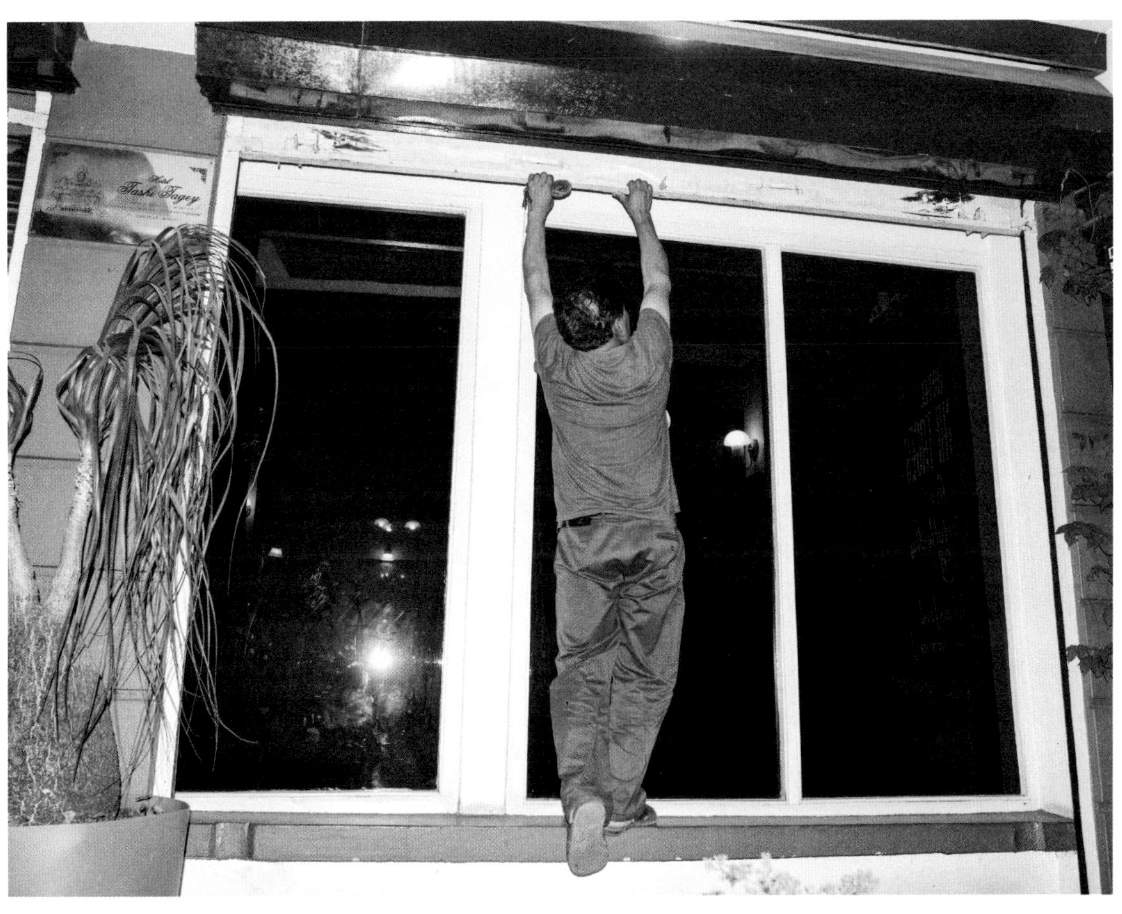

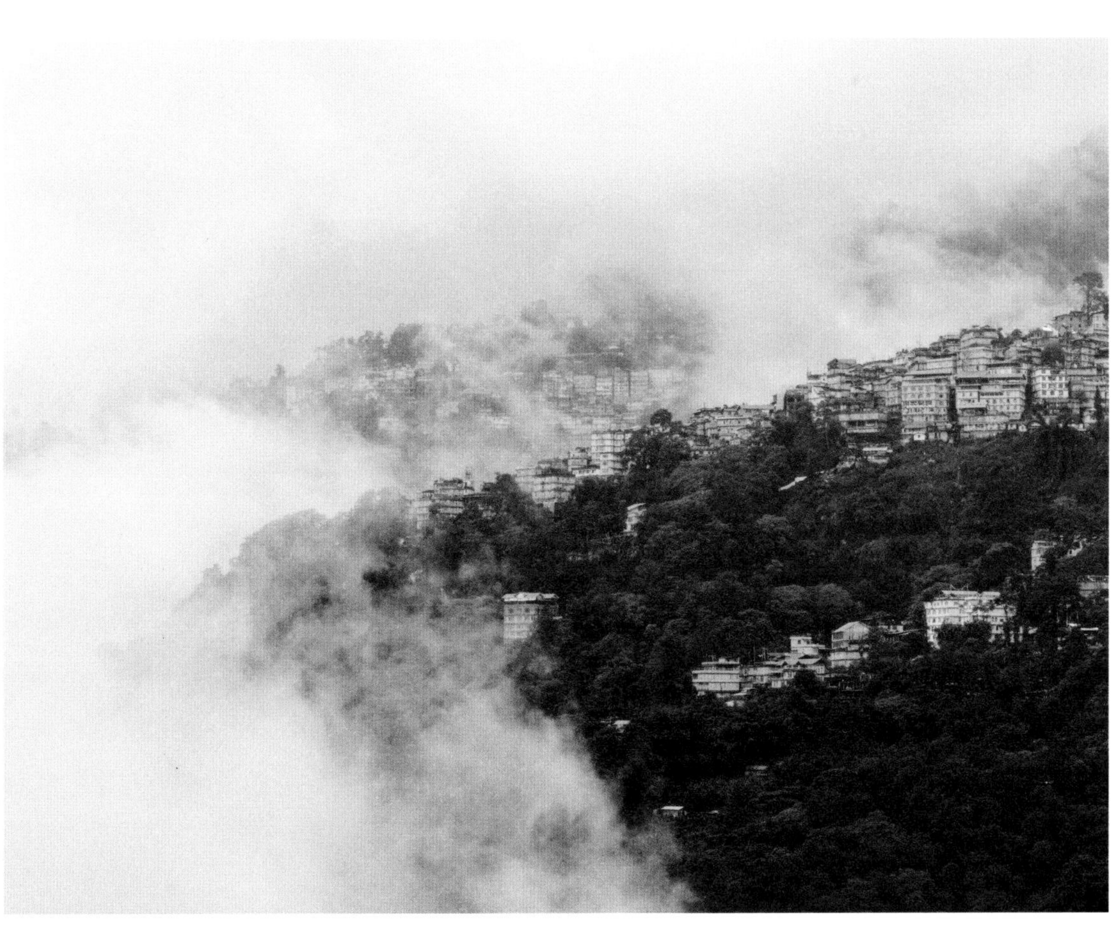

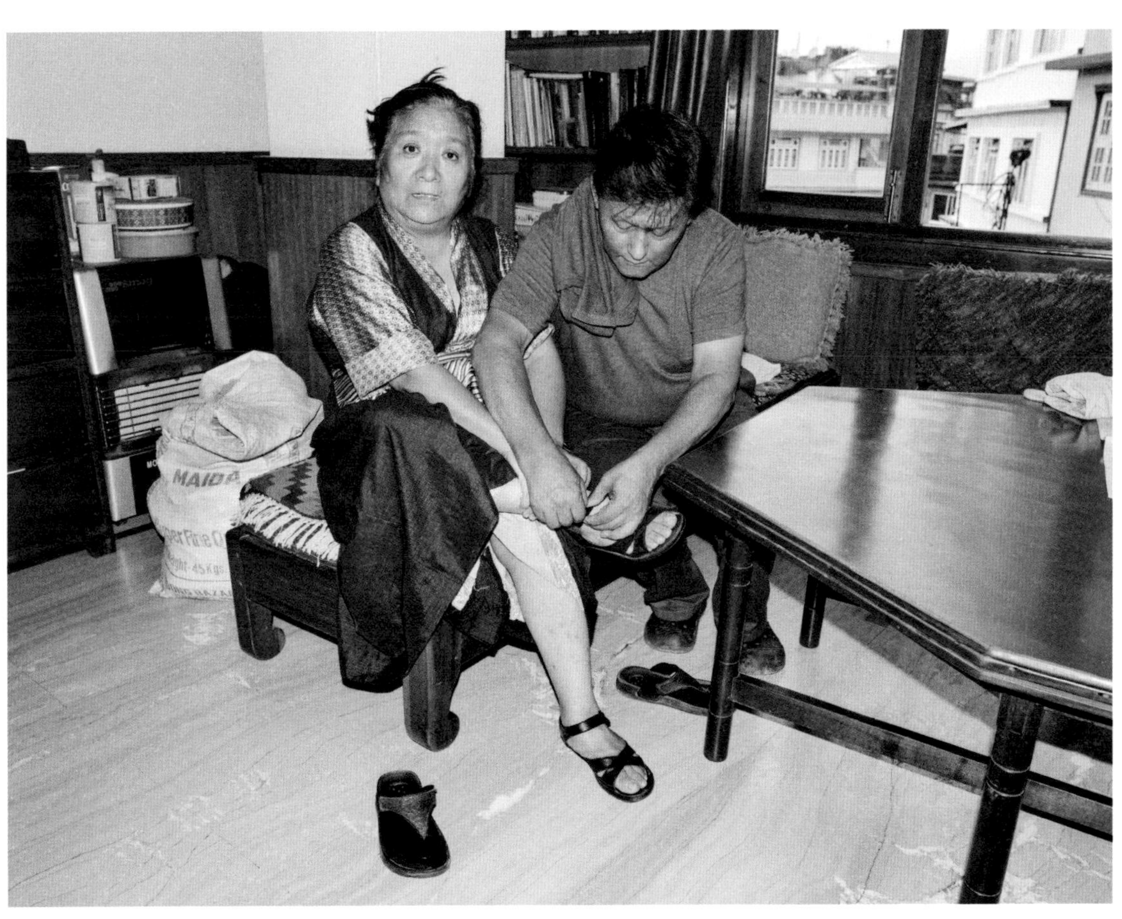

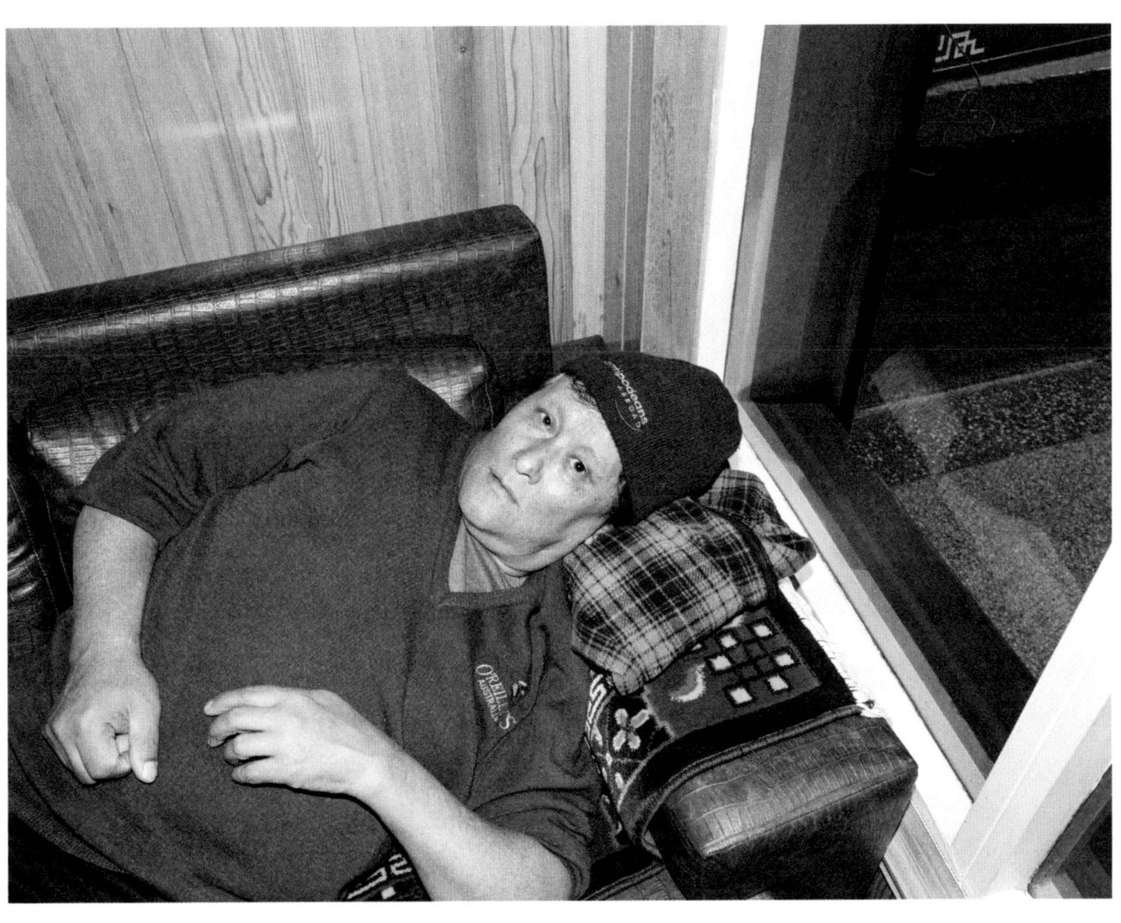

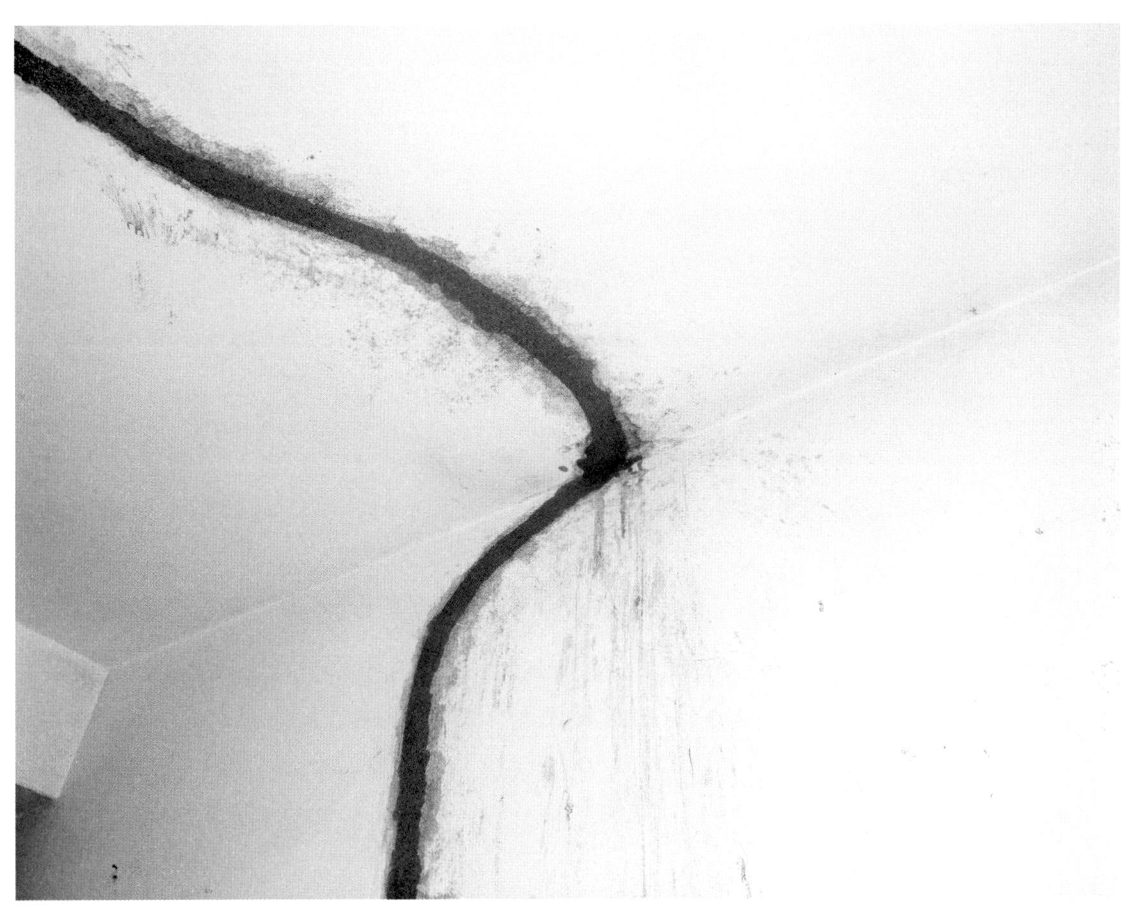

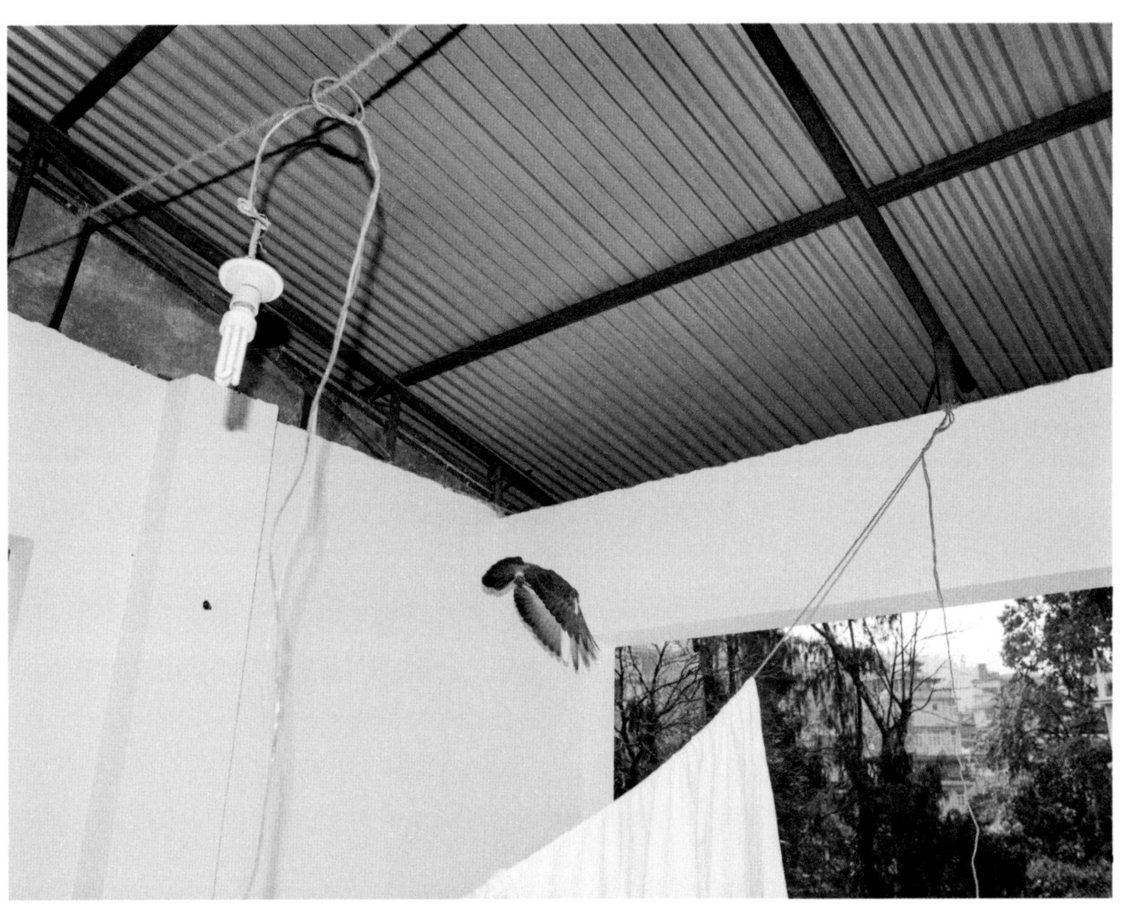

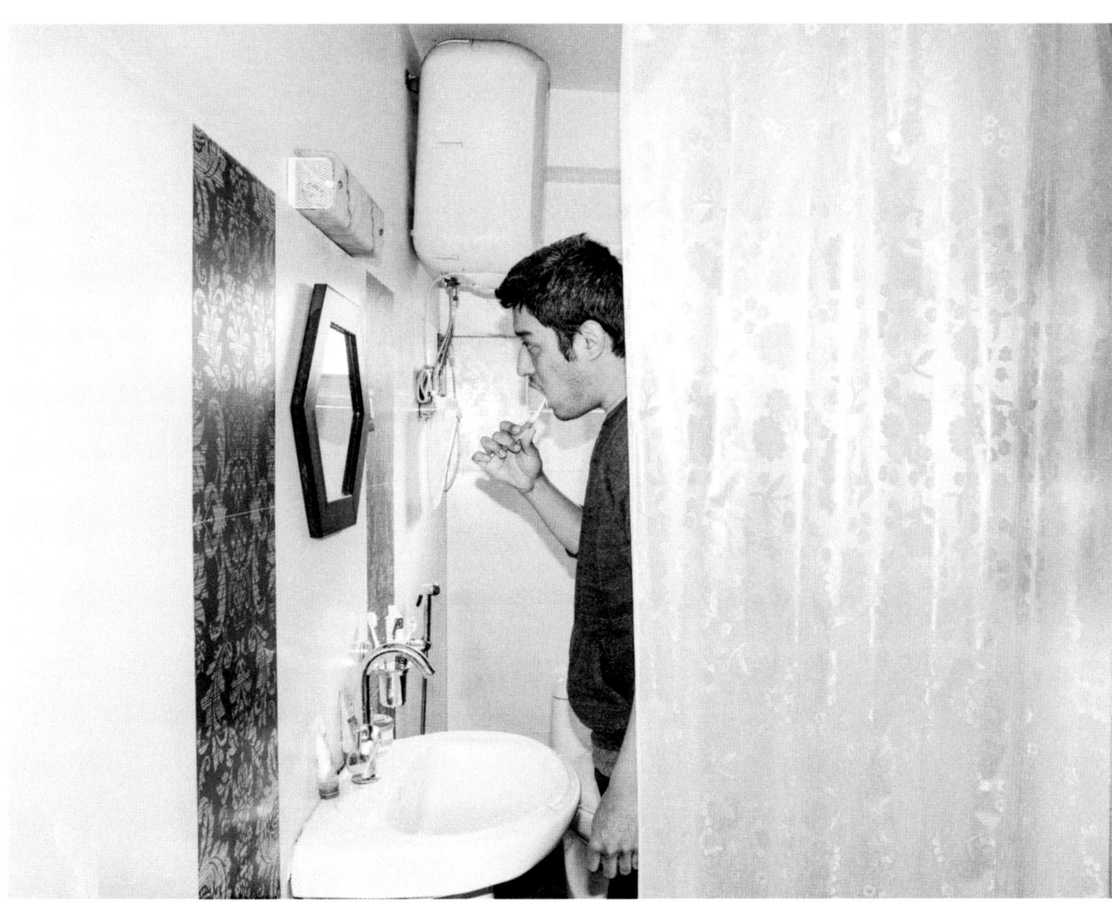

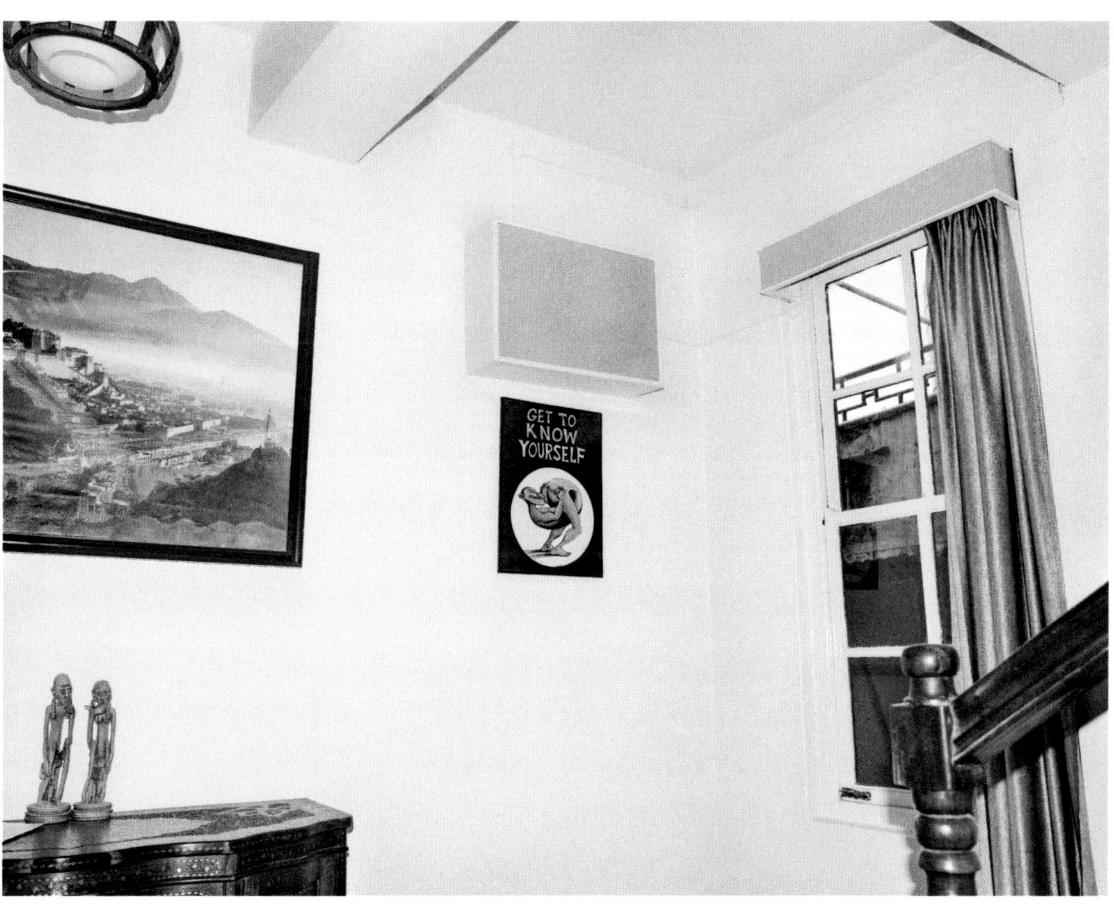
GET TO
KNOW
YOURSELF

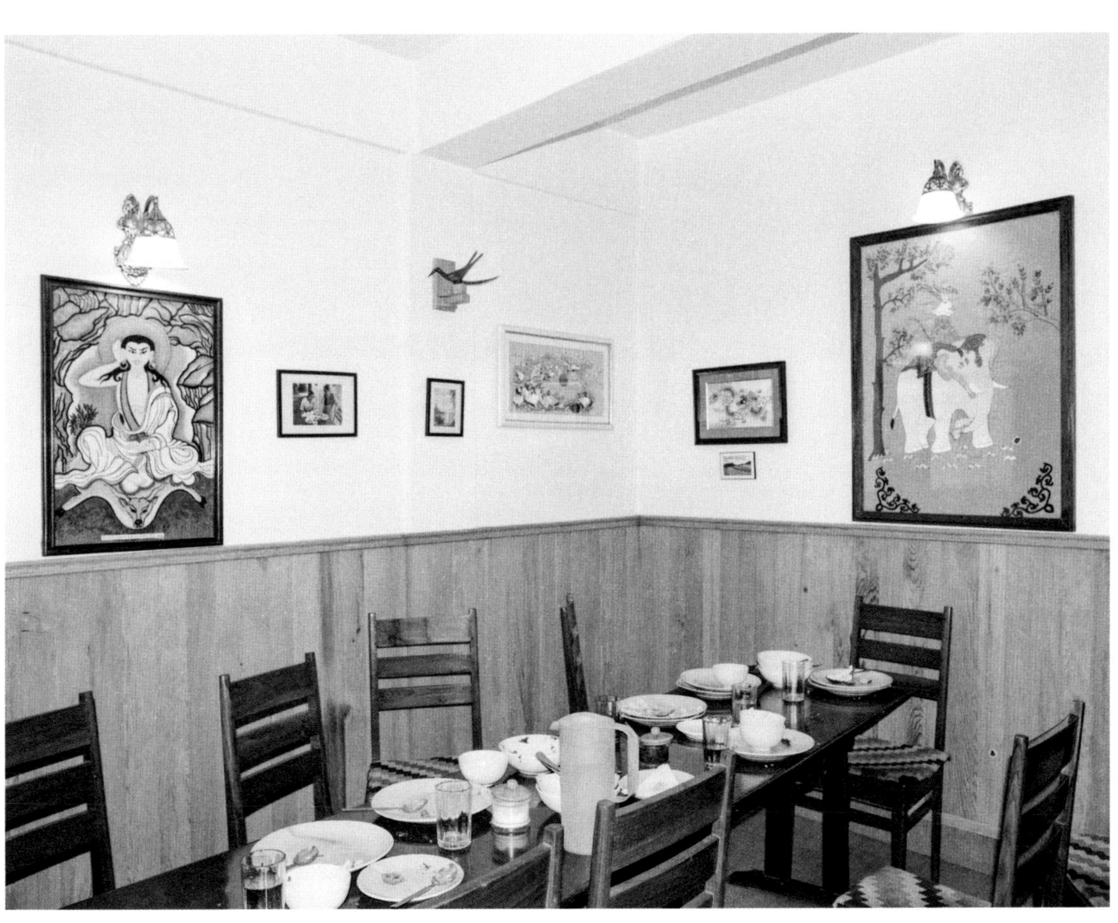

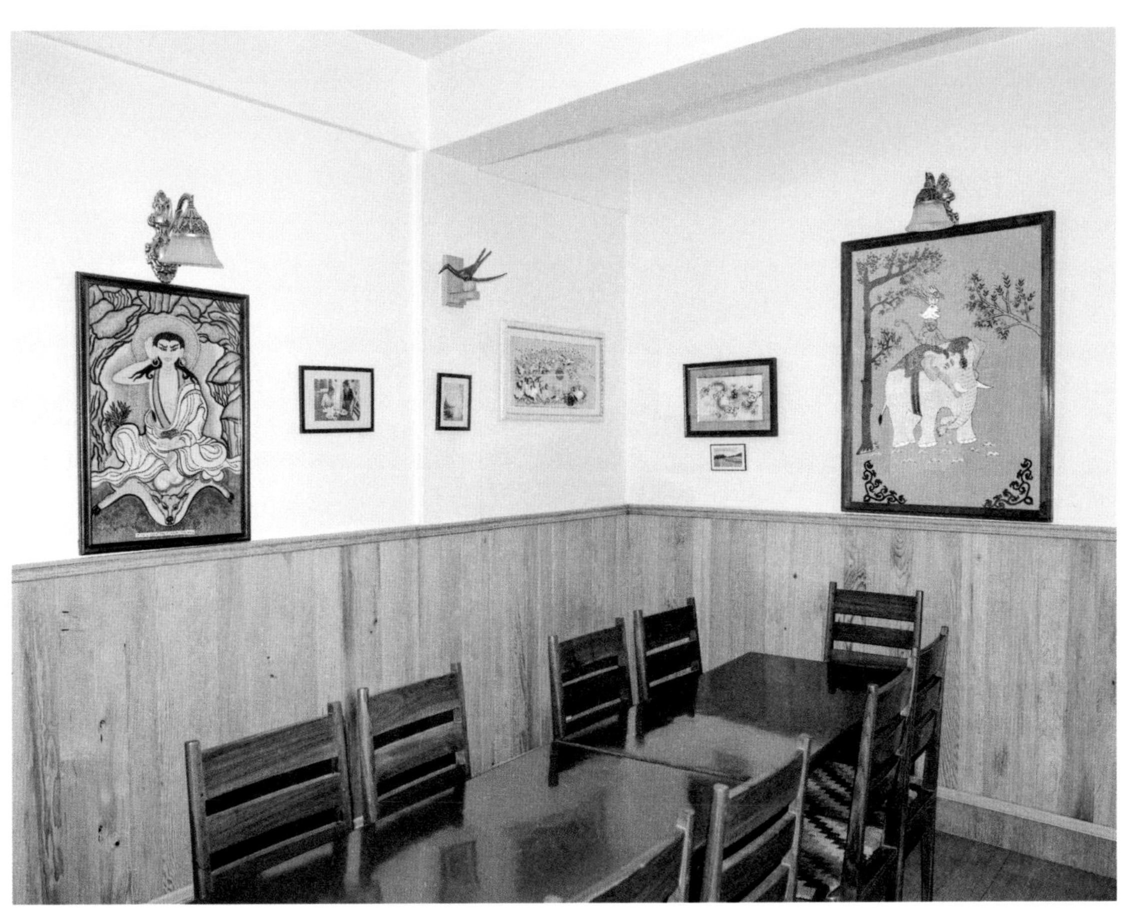

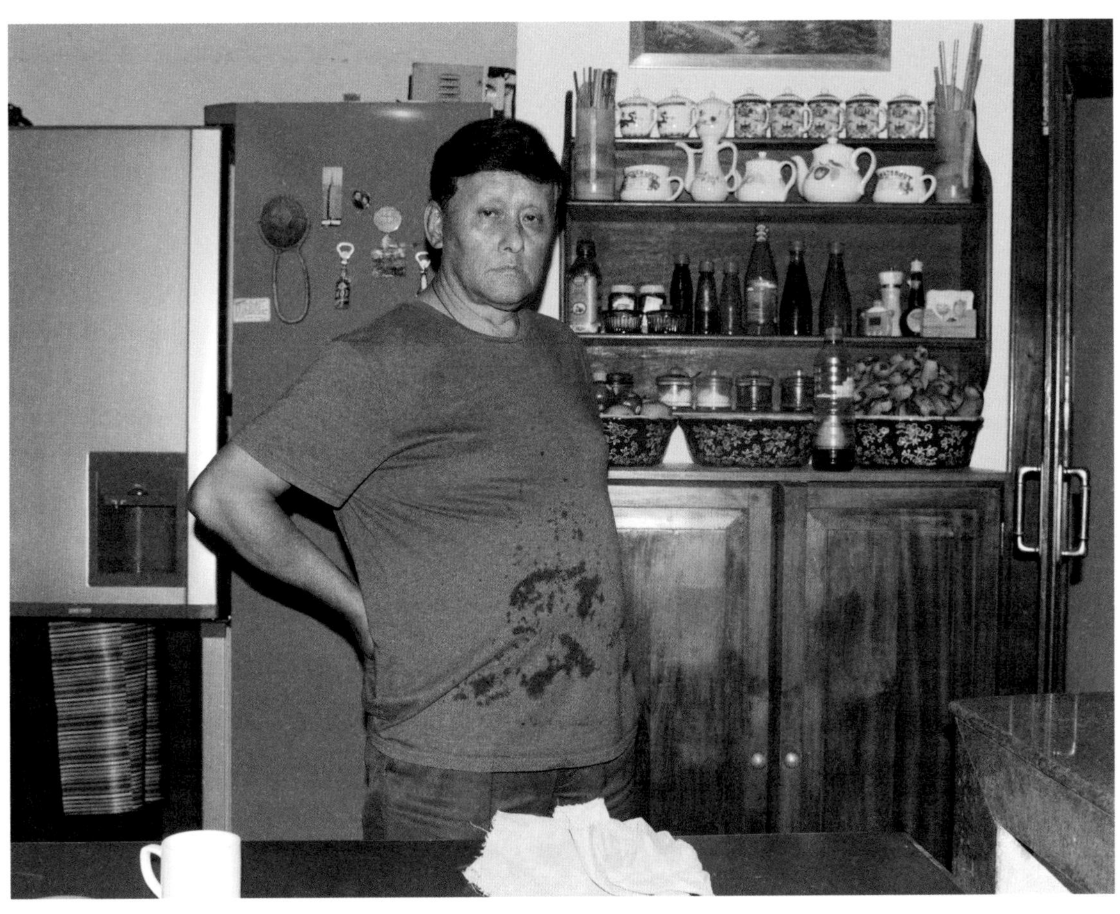

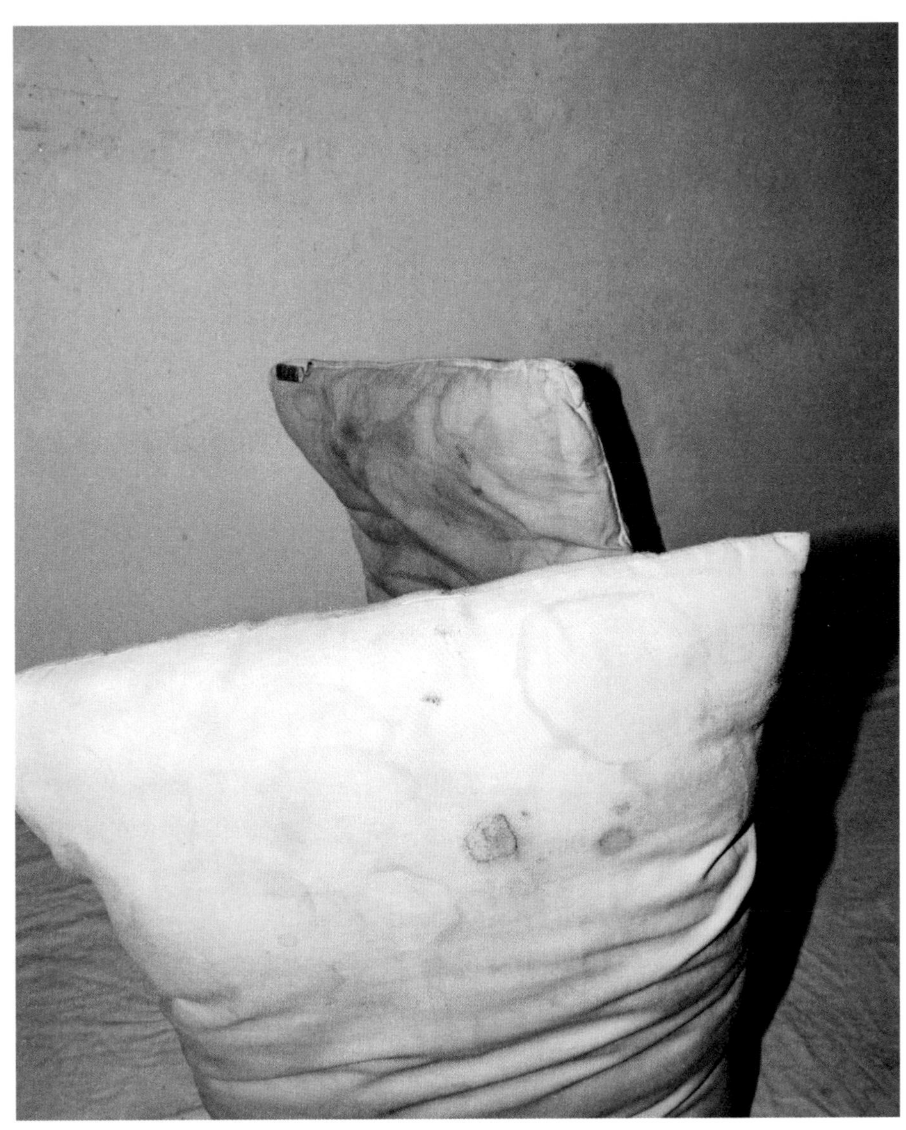

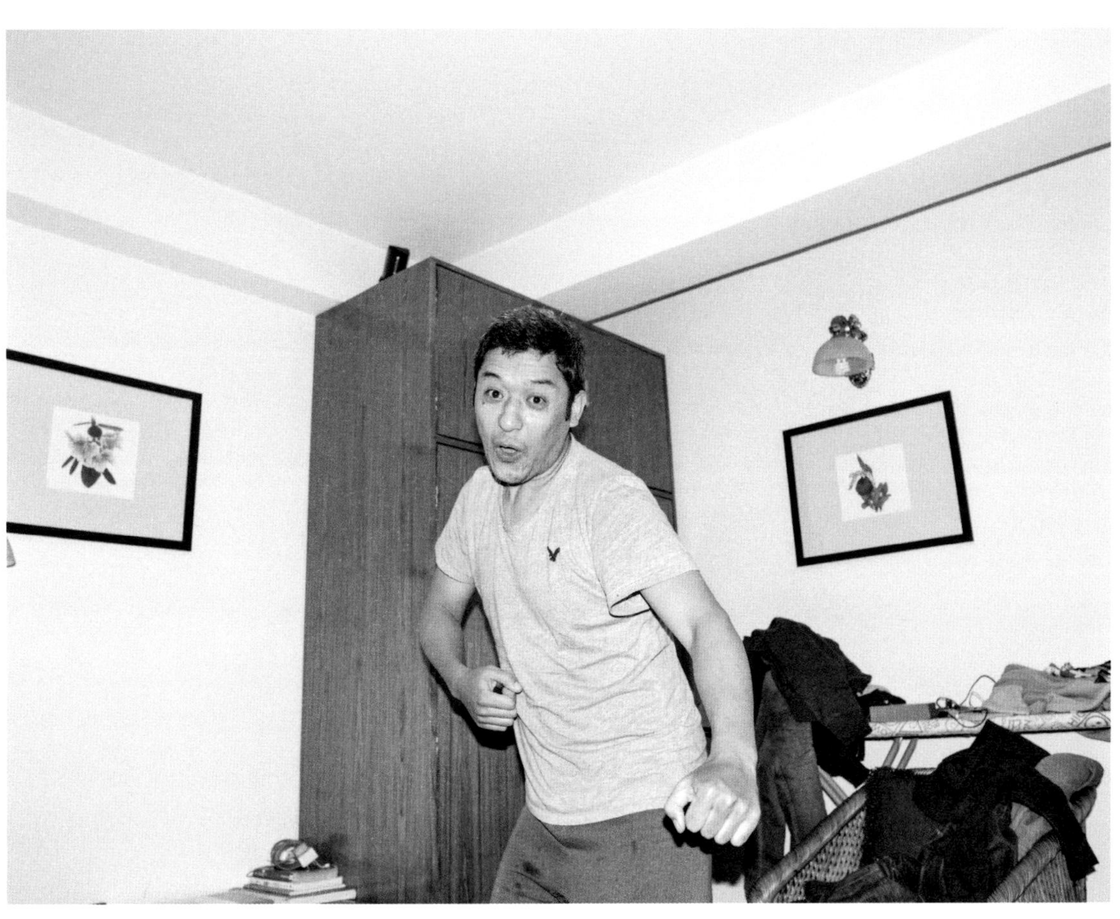

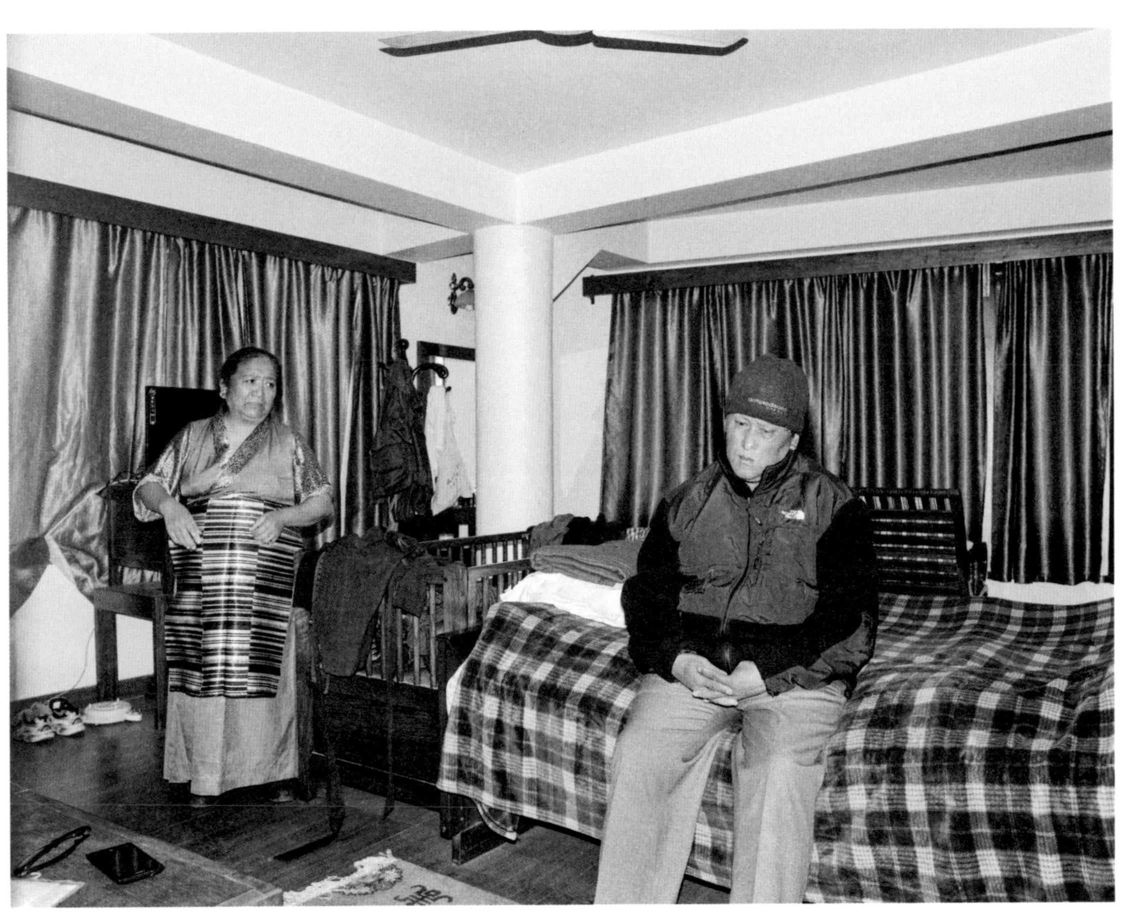

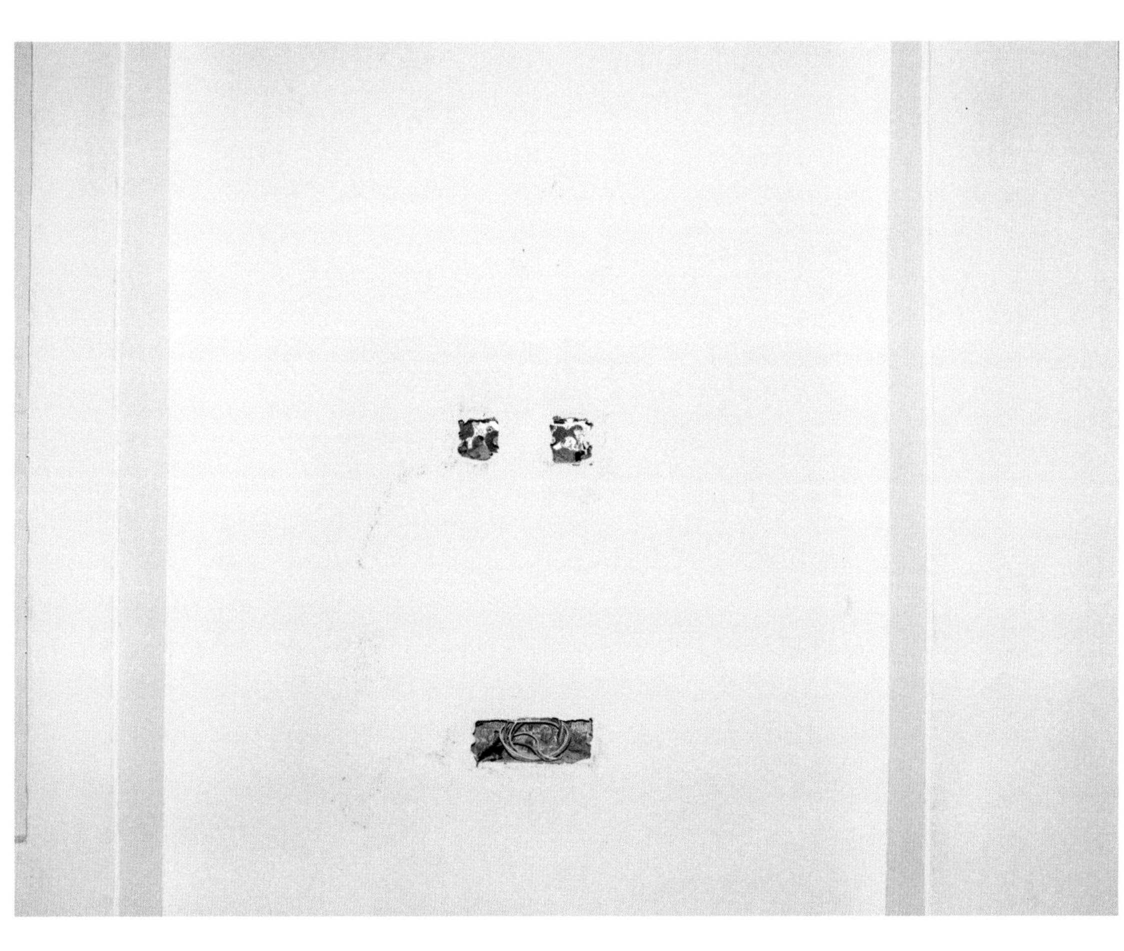

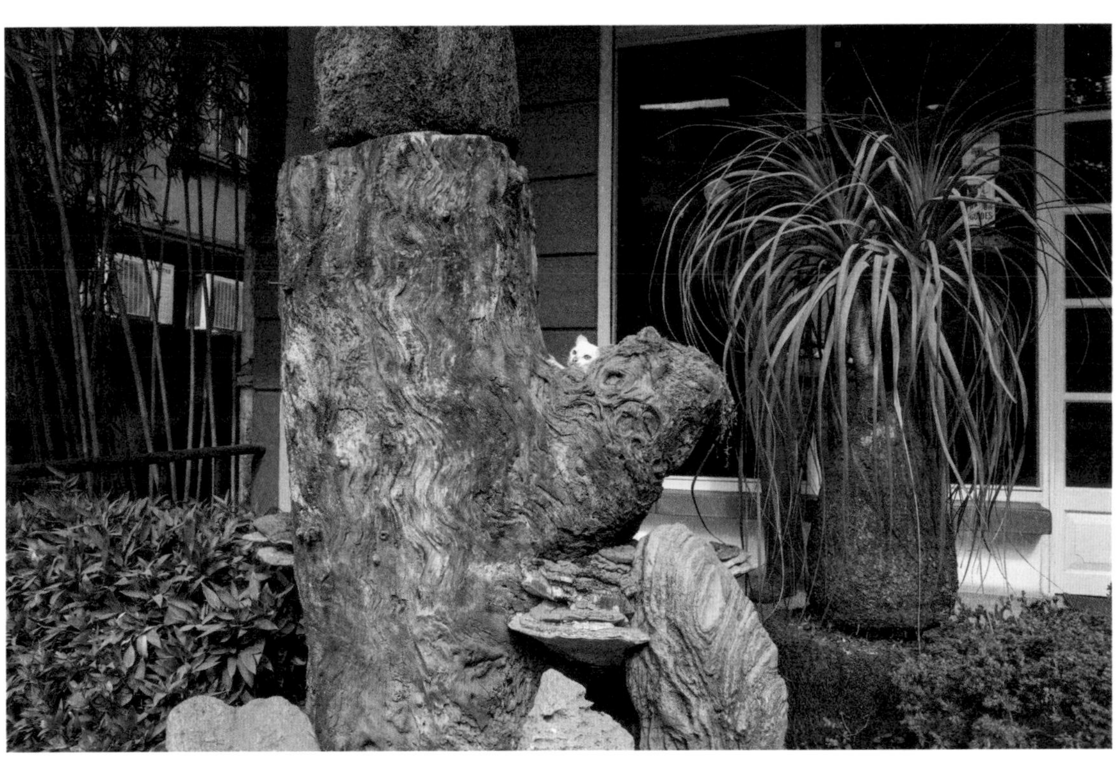

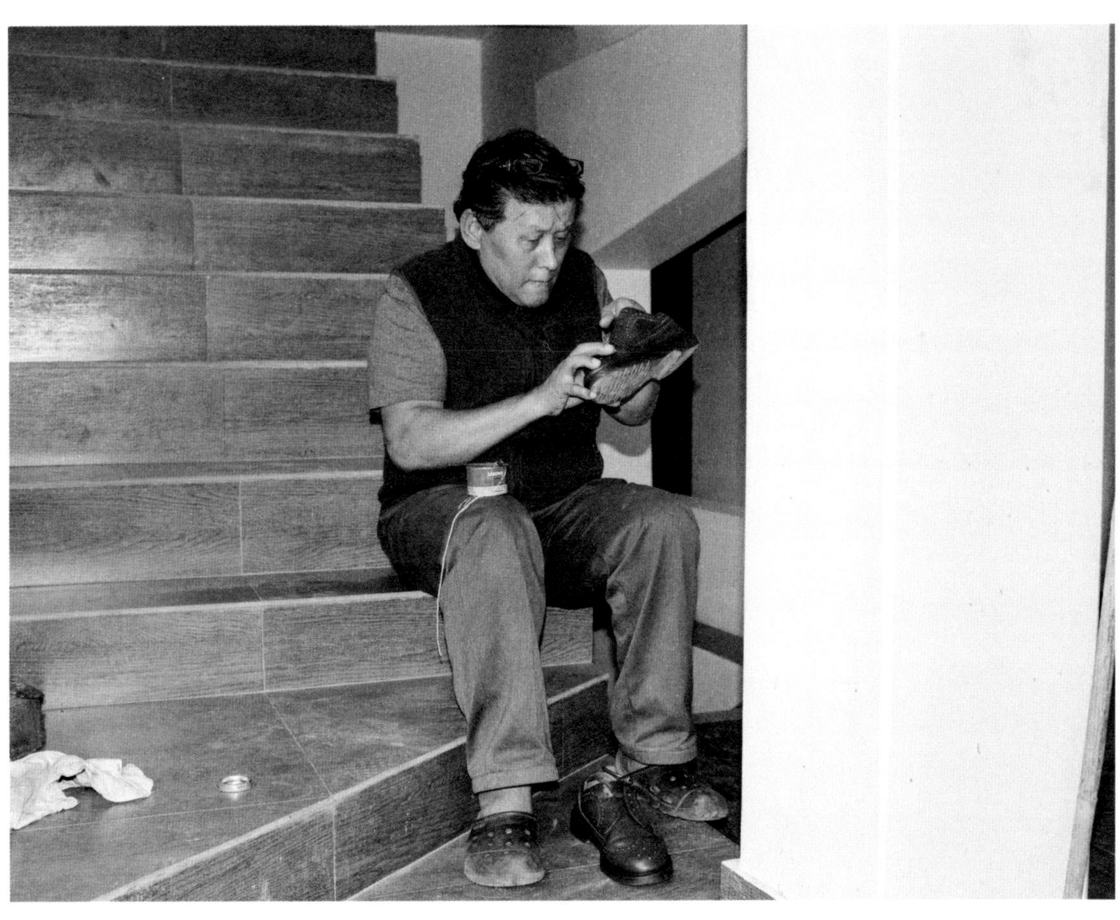

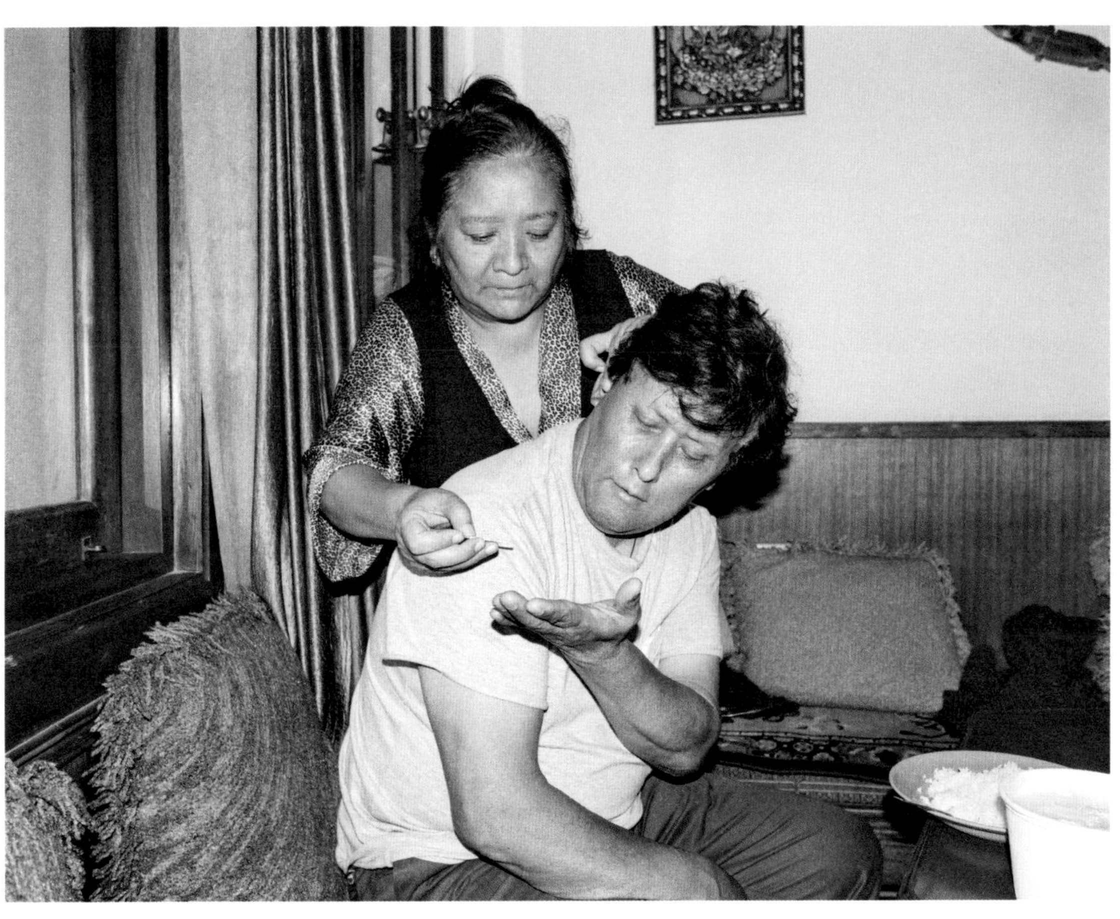

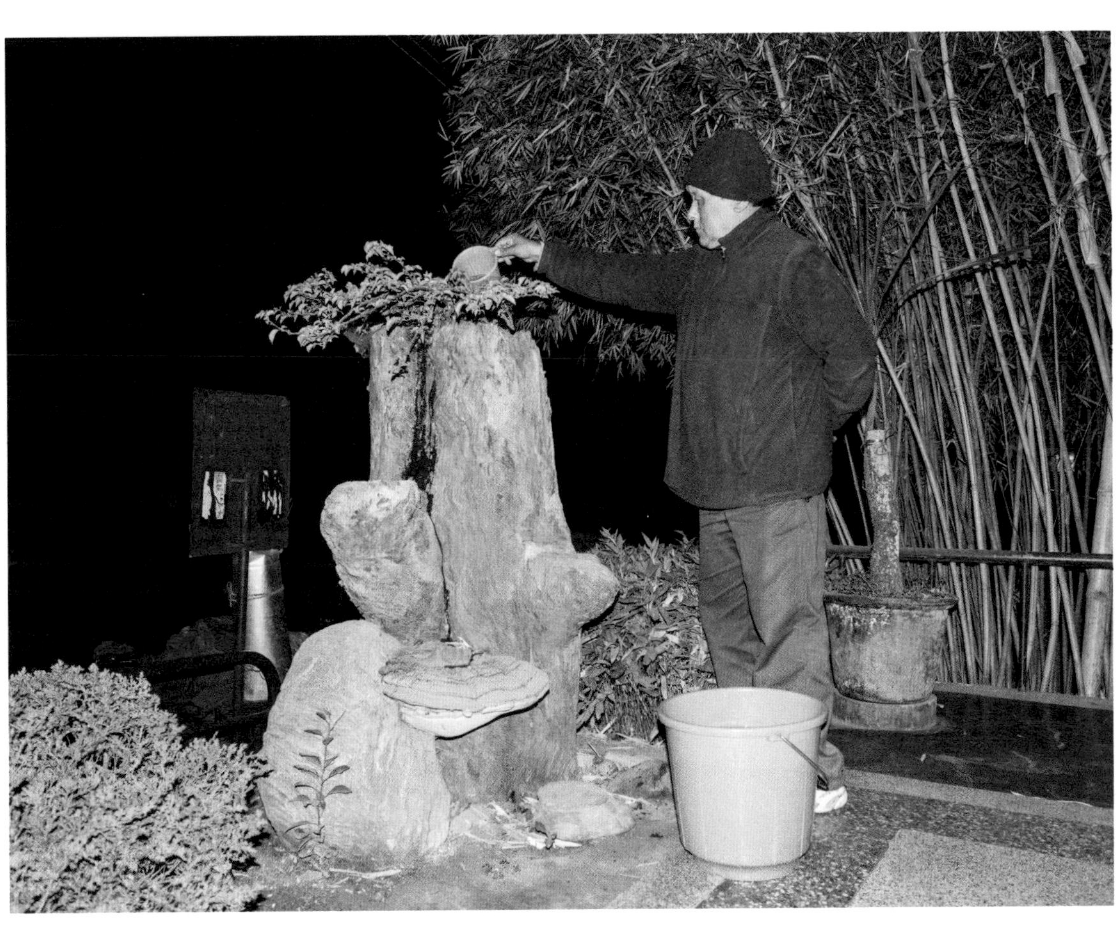

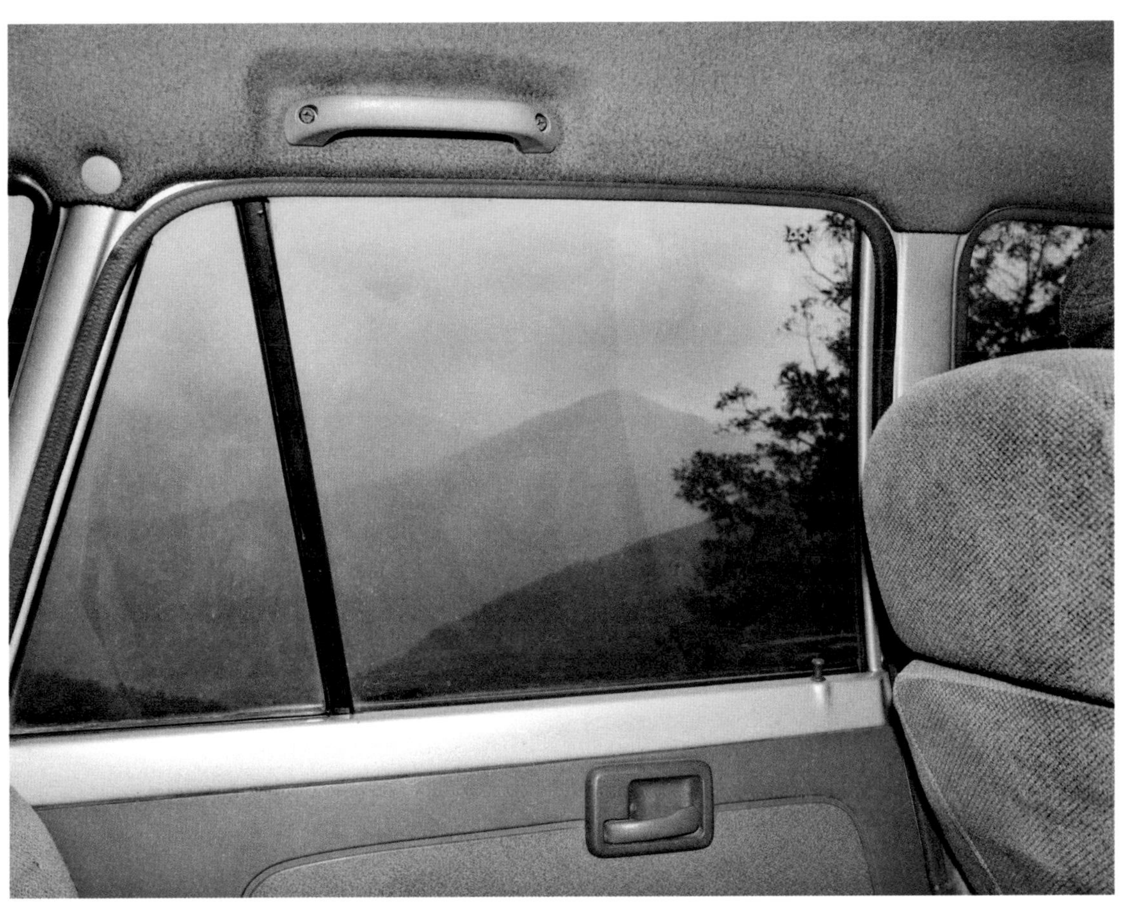

Tenzing Dakpa (b. 1985) lives and works between Sikkim, Goa and New Delhi. He is a second-generation Tibetan and was born in Sikkim, India. Dakpa first moved to New Delhi to study graphic design at the College of Art, University of Delhi (BFA, 2009) and then to the United States, where he studied at the Rhode Island School of Design (MFA Photography, 2016).

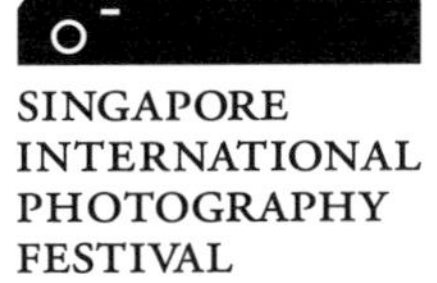

SINGAPORE
INTERNATIONAL
PHOTOGRAPHY
FESTIVAL

The Singapore International Photography Festival (SIPF) is a biennial gathering of minds from around the world with the common pursuit to advance the art and appreciation of photography. It aims to be a much needed arena for critical thought and academic discourse on photography in Southeast Asia. SIPF also functions as a key platform to discover, nurture, and propel Southeast Asian photographers onto the international stage. Through its satellite programmes, the festival hopes to engage the public and cultivate a larger audience.

The Photobook Award presented by SIPF seeks to uncover distinct voices in art and photography through the print form. The award also facilitates selected photographers in their creation of photobook publications. The winner of the SIPF Photobook Award 2018 is Tenzing Dakpa. He was selected by a jury panel of Ang Song Nian, Gerhard Steidl, Gwen Lee, Louise Fedotov-Clements, Sebastian Arthur Hau, Theseus Chan, Yanyou Diyuan, and Yumi Goto.

This photobook is generously made possible by Gerhard Steidl: "What I particularly like about this book is the absence of too much design. It's just pure photography printed on paper."

Special thanks to Nelson Chan, Steve Smith, Brian Ulrich,
Stanley Wolukau-Wanambwa, Kapil Das, Khem Fatimi, Brita Boruah,
Gerhard Steidl and his team.

First edition published in 2020

Book design: Tenzing Dakpa
Separations by Steidl image department
Production and printing: Steidl, Göttingen

Steidl
Düstere Straße 4 / 37073 Göttingen, Germany
Phone +49 (0551) 496060 / Fax +49 (0551) 4960649
mail@steidl.de
steidl.de

ISBN 978-3-95829-742-5
Printed in Germany by Steidl